Teaching:

The Heart of the Matter

By

John Smith

truth
BOOKS

ISBN 10: 1-58427-3690

ISBN 13: 978-1-58427-3691

Guardian of Truth Foundation
CEI Bookstore
220 S. Marion St., Athens, AL 35611
1-855-49-BOOKS or 1-855-492-6657
www.CEIbooks.com

Table of Contents

Dedication

This workbook is dedicated to
Pam Parker,
Sharon Baker,
and my wife, Diane Smith.

These three ladies represent the best of what it means to be a teacher.

I have learned much,
been encouraged,
and humbled
by their diligence
and love for teaching.

Introduction

I Would Gather Children

Some would gather money
    Along the path of life,
Some would gather roses,
    And the rest from worldly strife;
But I would gather children
    From among the thorns of sin,
I would seek a golden curl,
    And a freckled, toothless grin.
For money cannot enter
    In that land of endless day,
And roses that are gathered
    Soon will wilt along the way.
But, oh, the laughing children,
    As I cross the sunset sea,
And the gates swing wide to heaven
    I can take them in with me!

        – Author Unknown

You therefore, my son, be strong in the grace that is Christ Jesus. And the things that you have heard from me among any witnesses, commit these to faithful men who will be able to teach others also (2 Tim. 2:2).

What an incredible pleasure and fearful responsibility it is to be a teacher – molding young minds, reshaping old minds, changing lives and destinies. I can think of no other pursuit, except perhaps for being a parent, that is fraught with more potential pitfalls or more delightful rewards than teaching.

The fact that you have picked up this workbook indicates a desire on your part to improve your skills as a teacher. God bless you! I hope that in some small way I can help you accomplish that task.

I do not claim to know all there is to know about teaching or to be a perfect teacher (there was only one of those!). You may find yourself disagreeing with some of the things that I have to say. I hope that you do, for that will mean that you are thinking critically and taking the task of improving your teaching seriously. We need teachers who study and think for themselves.

I trust that I am committing these things to faithful men and women who will in turn use their new skills and knowledge to make the path to heaven a little clearer for those whom they teach.

In His Service,
John A. Smith

A Teacher's Prayer

I want to teach my students how to live this life on earth,
To face its struggles and its strife and to improve their work;
Not just a lesson in a book, or how the rivers flow,
But how to choose the proper path wherever they may go.
To understand eternal truth, and know the right from wrong,
And gather all the beauty of a flower and a song.
For if I help the world to grow in wisdom and in grace,
Then I shall feel that I have won and I have filled my place.
And so I ask your guidance, God, that I may do my part,
For character and confidence, and happiness of heart.

In Jesus name,
Amen

– Author Unknown

Lesson 1

Jesus: The Perfect Example of the Complete Teacher

"Never a man spake like this man" (Jn. 7:46).

Jesus is the perfect example of the complete teacher. Even His enemies marveled at His ability to teach (Jn. 7:46). The teaching of Jesus demonstrated keen insight into the students' hearts, comprehensive knowledge of the subject, and an exemplary attitude toward the mission of teaching. He desired to take His students deep into the Word so that they could see the underlying significance of the message. He was able to do so in a simple and easily understood manner. Jesus, the Master Teacher, took a heavenly message of eternal importance and lovingly expressed it so that the common man could understand. Like a living two-edged sword, His words cut deep into the hearts of the people.

What contributed to His success?

Jesus knew the Scriptures well. Having the Scriptures engraved on His heart, He was able to call on them when needed. When confronted by Satan in the wilderness, Jesus was able to fend off temptation by an appeal to the Word (see Matt. 4:1-11). Three times He replied, "It is written" and quoted appropriate Scripture. He knew the Scriptures far better than the most learned of Israel. He often appealed to the prophecies of Scripture to establish His identity. Without an accurate knowledge of the Scriptures, He could not have taught others effectively. The simple reality is that one cannot teach what one does not know.

It is true that you and I will never know as much about the Scriptures as the "Incarnate Word," but we don't have to! Our challenge is to learn as much as we can and always be growing in "the grace and knowledge of our Lord and Savior Jesus Christ" (2 Pet. 3:18). We are to add to our faith, virtue and knowledge which are to be abounding and increasing (2 Pet. 1:5-8). If the teacher is willing to take heed unto himself and his doctrine, he can save himself and those he teaches (1 Tim. 4:16). Every teacher needs to keep a love for learning alive within his heart. There will never come a time when we can be content with our present storehouse of biblical knowledge. The more we learn about the Scriptures, the more we resemble the "Master Teacher."

Jesus had the proper attitude toward the Scriptures. He viewed all Scripture as the inspired, infallible Word of God. He affirmed that the Scriptures could not be broken (Jn. 10:35) and that they all had to be fulfilled (Lk. 24:44; Matt. 5:17-18). He viewed the Old Testament Scriptures as historically accurate, accepting as historical Jonah and his experience in the great fish (Matt. 12:40). He accepted the historicity of the Genesis account of creation when He quoted Genesis 2 to establish God's unchanged marriage law (Matt. 19:4-6).

To be an effective teacher of God's Word today, a person must accept all of the Scripture as having been inspired by God. The effective teacher will receive the Scriptures in the same manner as Jesus and the Thessalonian brethren: "And for this reason we also thank God that when you received from us the word of God's message, you accepted it not as the word of men, but for what it really is, the word of God, which also performs its work in you who believe" (1 Thess. 2:13). The effective teacher recognizes that the holy men of God did not write of their own inspiration, but "men moved by the Holy Spirit spoke from God" (2 Pet. 1:21). If we share the confidence and enthusiasm of Jesus toward the Scriptures, we possess one of the essential qualities of an effective teacher.

Jesus had the proper attitude toward his students. He knew the nature and attitudes of people (Jn. 2:24-25; 10:14). He loved them deeply to the point of sacrificing His own life for them (Jn. 15:12-13). He was interested in their needs (Matt. 15:32) and prayed for them often (Jn. 17:9, 20-21). He listened to His students to find out what their perceptions were and what they knew (Matt. 16:14-16). Jesus was a "people person."

Whether or not we ever engage in the good work of teaching, these characteristics of Jesus should be fresh in our lives. Even if we do take on the awesome responsibility of being a Bible teacher, these characteristics are indispensable. The students will learn more and respond with greater enthusiasm if they know that we care for them.

Jesus had the proper objective in teaching. The Son of man came to "save that which was lost" (Matt. 18:11). As "the way, the truth and the life," He taught that others might come to the Father (Jn. 14:6). He did not intend to "make a name for Himself" or rally a personal following. He did not teach to satisfy His own ego. When Jesus took aim with the "Sword," He had His target clearly in view – the saving of lost souls.

Whether we teach the youngest or the oldest of students, our objective will always be these. Whether we "lift up the hands that hang down," strengthen the "feeble knees," or make "straight paths" for the students' feet (Heb. 12:12-13), we do so in an effort to secure the salvation of their souls. No nobler objective could ever be pursued. When you share the Word of God with someone, you help them obtain a reward that transcends this life. The effects of your teaching will not end at the grave, but reap an abundant harvest in the last great day.

Follow the Master into the Field

While teaching in Perea, Jesus encountered a certain ruler who desired eternal life: "And a certain ruler asked him, saying, 'Good Master, what shall I do to obtain eternal life?' And Jesus said unto him, 'Why do you call Me good? No one is good, except God alone. You know the commandments, do not commit adultery, do not murder, do not steal, do not bear false witness, honor your father and mother.' And he said, 'All these things have I kept from my youth up.' Now when Jesus heard these things, he said unto him, 'One thing you still lack; sell all that you possess, and distribute it to the poor, and you shall have treasure in heaven: and come, follow me.' And when he heard this, he was very sorrowful: for he was very rich" (Lk. 18:18-23)

Jesus began by getting the man's attention, "Why callest thou Me good?" Jesus was a master at using questions to gain the interest of His audience. He would often ask questions designed to perplex the student or cause him to look deep into his own heart and motives. There was no need for a fancy show or gimmicks to gain and maintain the man's attention. Jesus simply relied upon mental activity.

Jesus began with what the man already knew. He began from a point of common understanding and agreement – the commandments. It was then that Jesus took the man to where he needed to be.

In this teaching situation was Jesus a failure? The man went away sorrowful and unconverted. What did Jesus have to show for this effort? Some might be tempted to suggest that Jesus was a failure since He did not achieve His goal of penetrating and changing this man's heart. However, to suggest such is to miss the point of teaching. Jesus sowed the seed. Each heart had to determine what he would do with the seed. As a teacher, Jesus was responsible for the sowing of the seed, not its reception.

A chance meeting with a Samaritan woman at a well near Sychar provided Jesus with an opportunity to teach (see Jn. 4:5-29). This woman came out of the city for the very ordinary task of fetching a jug of water. Given the social chasm between the Samaritans and the Jews, this encounter was quite unusual. Jesus took the time to teach a woman who would have been considered by the Jews of less importance than a dog. Jesus did not judge the worthiness of the student. When He saw a thirsting soul, He moved to quench the spiritual need.

Jesus began this quest for spiritual knowledge with something as ordinary as a cup of water. He viewed the every day situations of life not as ordinary, but as momentous opportunities to teach spiritual lessons. With a cup of water and an appropriate appeal, Jesus captured the attention of this woman. He offered her "living water" and a chance to thirst no more! He got her curious, involved, and eager to learn.

In capturing the attention of this woman and teaching her about the "living water," Jesus did not compromise any principle of truth. He reminded her of God's disapproval of the Samaritans when He said, "You worship that which you do not know" (Jn. 4:22). He would have done her no favor if He ignored her faults.

The response of this worldly Samaritan woman was tremendous. She left her water pot by the well and rushed back to the city to boldly proclaim the arrival of the Messiah. As a result of her announcement many of the Samaritans went out to Jesus and were filled with faith. The teaching of one led to the opportunity to teach many.

Conclusion

There were many other characteristics which Jesus had that made Him a masterful teacher. Sue Crabtree, in her book *Let's Be Great Teachers,* lists the following attributes which helped make Jesus the greatest Bible teacher:

- Was a great storyteller (Matt. 13:1-11, 24-33 or any of His parables)
- Used visual aids in His teaching (Matt. 11:1-4; 14:19; 16:2-3)
- Taught the application of His lesson (Man. 12:46-50)
- Took time to evaluate the learning of His students (Man. 13:51)
- Took time to pray in private (Matt. 14:23)
- Above all He lived out what He taught.

Follow Up and Discussion

1. How did a comprehensive knowledge of God's Word help Jesus become a masterful teacher? _____

   _____

2. What practical steps can you take to increase in Bible knowledge? _____

   _____

3. Summarize Jesus' attitude toward the Scriptures: _____

   _____

   _____

4. What do the following passages tell us about God's Word?
   a. 2 Timothy 3:16-17 _____
   b. 2 Peter 1:2-4 _____
   c. 1 Corinthians 2:6-13 _____
5. What attitude did Jesus take toward His students and how did this affect His teaching? _____

   _____

6. What was the constant goal of Jesus in all of His teaching? _____
    _____

7. How will a person's teaching be affected if he does not have the right goal?
    _____
    _____

8. What lessons about teaching can we learn from Jesus' encounter with the
    rich young ruler? _____
    _____

9. What lessons about teaching can we learn from Jesus' encounter with the
    Samaritan woman? _____
    _____

10. Of the characteristics listed by Crabtree, which do you think is the most im-
    portant? _____
    _____

Look Into Your Heart. . .

As you compare yourself as a teacher to Jesus, in what areas are you most like
Him? _____
_____
_____
_____

In what areas are you most lacking? _____
_____
_____
_____
_____
_____

Lesson 2

Teaching: "The Heart of the Matter"

Remember not only to say the right thing in the right place, but far more difficult still, to leave unsaid the wrong thing at the tempting time. – Ben Franklin

The importance of teaching the ways and laws of God cannot be stressed enough. In teaching God's Word, we are preparing people for a lifetime of service and the judgment to follow. As a teacher you face an awesome task. In fact James cautions, "Let not many of you become teachers, my brethren, knowing that as such we shall incur a stricter judgment" (Jas. 3:1, NASV). Becoming a teacher is a matter, as the "marrying man" puts it, "not to be entered into lightly or unadvisedly." Everyone who assumes the role of Bible teacher shall receive greater judgment, if what is taught is faulty. Teachers undertake to convey God's Word in the way in which God wants it conveyed; God will judge them on that score. But, to avoid entirely the responsibility of teaching might in some ways be comparable to the person who says, "I fear to become a Christian lest I should backslide and my latter state as a sinner be worse than my present state as a sinner." Yes brethren, teaching is an awesome responsibility, but it is one that, if faced correctly, will provide some of life's greatest rewards.

Satan is attempting to fill people's minds with all kinds of garbage. Far too many people drink freely without restraint from the "cesspool" of the world. We must be willing to fight back and fill their minds with the good things of God's Word. Those whom we teach are engaged in a battle with Satan every day. We must be willing to instruct them in the use of the "sword of the Spirit" (Eph. 6:17). We must be willing to provide for them access to and instruction in the use of the "water of life." Teaching someone math, spelling, or geography will prepare him for temporal success, but teaching him God's Word will prepare him for eternal success.

The Importance of Teaching

The importance of teaching can be easily seen in the works of Deity. God, by nature, is a teacher. Since the beginning of man's existence, God has been involved in imparting knowledge to man. In the Garden, after the flood, at Sinai, and beyond God taught man how to love, treat others, and serve Him. He unselfishly shared His wisdom with man.

Jesus is the "Master Teacher." He came to earth to reveal God and was constantly involved in teaching situations. In John 4 He used a chance meeting with a woman at a well to teach her of His mission as the Son of God. He taught a large crowd of people from the vantage point of a small Galilean hill. He went into the home of Zaccheaus, a tax collector, to teach him. With simplicity and mystery He revealed heaven's secrets. He took advantage of every opportunity to declare the will of the Father. If we desire to walk in the steps of the Master, we must be about the Master's business – teaching.

To be godly, we must teach the will of the Lord. We must allow it to radiate daily from our hearts to the world, our children, and those we teach in a classroom setting.

The importance of teaching can be seen in God's commission to the nation of Israel: "And these words, which I am commanding you this day, shall be on your heart: And you shall teach them diligently to your sons, and shall talk of them when you sit in your house, and when you walk by the way, and when you lie down, and when you rise up. And you shall bind them as a sign upon your hand, and they shall be as frontals on your forehead. And you shall write them on the doorposts of your house, and on your gates" (Deut. 6:6-9). The laws were to be diligently taught to the children after the "teachers" had lived them. The parents were to use formal and informal teaching settings to impart this knowledge to their children. This teaching would result in the children coming closer to God and their prosperity in the land.

The importance of teaching can be seen in the Great Commission (Matt. 28:18-20). Teaching is one of the most fundamental responsibilities of every Christian. Even if we could not find a passage instructing Christians to teach, their love for the Lord and joy of salvation should compel them to share it with others. If we are filled with Christ; if we have crucified ourselves that Christ might live in us (Gal. 2:20), then no power on earth can close our hearts or shut our mouths.

Teaching is essential to one becoming a Christian (Rom. 10:17). Have you ever met a person whom you did not desire to see become a Christian? If you desire to see the children of your congregation become Christians, then you must be about the task of teaching. Teaching is essential to one remaining a Christian. In order for a person to keep the commandments of God, he must know what he is to observe. How can he know except someone teach him (Rom. 10:14-15)?

Finally, the importance of teaching can be seen in the destructiveness of ignorance. Hosea lamented that his people were being destroyed for a lack of knowledge (Hos. 4:6). The problem was not that there was no source of knowledge. God had not forgotten to tell them how He wanted them to live. The problem was that they had rejected knowledge and thus God was going to reject them. Ignorance is destructive. If we fail to teach the Word of God diligently then we become contributors to ignorance and the condemnation of souls.

Preparation of the Teacher's Heart (Deut. 6:4-6)

The teacher's heart must be wholly and completely devoted to God: "And you shall love the Lord your God with all your heart, and with all your soul, and with all your might" (v. 5). God is deserving of our undivided devotion and love. The whole of man is to be yielded to God in holy and devout affection. Such needs to be communicated to those whom we teach. The teacher cannot communicate what is not present. We need to be teaching and preparing our children to love the Lord with all their heart, soul, mind, and strength (Matt. 22:36-38). But how can this be accomplished unless they see it alive in us? Our service as teachers must begin with dedicated and prepared hearts. Teaching from a prepared, devoted, and excited heart will bring great results and great rewards.

The teacher's heart must be filled with the Word of God: "And these words, which I am commanding you this day, shall be on your heart" (v. 6). Jesus said that out of the "abundance of the heart the mouth speaks" (Matt. 12:34). If we intend to teach the Word of God, then we need to fill our hearts with it. Those whom we teach need to see the example of one who is dedicated to the Word and who has acquired a working knowledge of it. This is not to suggest that we must have a super abundance of knowledge before we teach or that we must be able to answer every question. However, we cannot teach if we are not growing and increasing in knowledge.

The teacher's heart is to be guided by the Word of God (vv. 8-9). The laws were to be on their hands. It was to guard and direct the actions of the hands. The laws were to be on their foreheads. They were to guard and direct the thoughts and direction of the people. The laws were to be on their doorposts. They were to be in plain view where all could easily see and guide the family within. As teachers we need to show forth an example of those whose lives and actions are guided by the Word of God. Our actions, thoughts, direction in life, and homes should reflect the purity of the Word of God.

In the quiet and privacy of your own home take a few minutes to reflect upon the condition of your heart. Is it prepared to teach the Word of God? Is it prepared to "rightly divide the Word of Truth"? Does your life reflect a heart that is pure and wholly devoted to God?

Please take a few moments to complete the following checklist of personal traits that are important for teachers. Don't be too hard on yourself. Be honest enough to give yourself credit for the good things that you have to bring into the classroom. Be honest enough to recognize the areas where you need to improve.

Personal Traits Checklist for Teachers
O = Outstanding S = Satisfactory N = Needs improvement X = Non-existent

_____ 1. Love the Lord with my whole heart,
_____ 2. Love and appreciate children.
_____ 3. Willing to make sacrifices to properly prepare.
_____ 4. Have willingness and desire to study Bible.
_____ 5. Considerate of the feelings of others.
_____ 6. Adaptable to change without getting irritable.
_____ 7. Live with integrity that will not compromise what is taught.
_____ 8. Have the ability to take criticism without becoming bitter.
_____ 9. Patient with children.
_____ 10. Confident in ability to work well with children.

Continued Growth is Essential for the Teacher

In Luke 2:52, we have an account of the four-fold growth of our Lord. He grew spiritually (in favor with God), mentally (in wisdom), socially (in favor with men), and physically (in stature). As teachers we need to be involved in a continual growth process in all of these areas (with perhaps the exception of growing physically – some of us can't afford to grow physically any more!).

Spiritual Growth

Spiritual growth comes only with desire and commitment. All Christians, but especially teachers, need to ask themselves, "What kind of Christian am I?" and "What kind of Christian do I want to be?" Upon answering these questions, the teacher needs to initiate a program for personal spiritual growth. From deep within our hearts we need to radiate a special attitude toward the priorities of life that indicates we are a person striving for spiritual maturity. The teacher's heart and treasure need to be clearly focused on things spiritual in nature and eternal in consequence. It has been said, "You teach little by what you say, more by what you do, and the most by what you are."

Mental Growth

Mental growth requires sacrifice. As teachers we must be willing to sacrifice the appropriate amount of time to our own personal study of God's Word. The teacher must be constantly increasing in knowledge and application of the Word. We must stand on our own knowledge. We cannot rely or depend on someone else's knowledge. As teachers we will need the "tools of the trade" and know how to use them properly. You would do well to begin building your own Bible reference library. "Grow in the grace and knowledge of our Lord and Savior Jesus Christ."

Social Growth

Teachers need to be able to get along with and communicate with others. The Bible class teacher needs to grow in his compassion, love, and involvement with others. The teacher in a Bible class can help his students grow socially. However, it needs to be understood that class time is not a time for socialization. Such can be accomplished by the teacher talking with his students after class and in their homes. Visiting students in their homes and having them in your home can foster your and their social growth.

Follow Up and Discussion

1. What is the point that James is making in 3:1? _____
    _____
    How should this affect the attitude with which a person begins to teach?
    _____
    _____

2. How can one come to appreciate the importance of teaching from each of the following:
    a. Work of Deity: _____
    b. Commission to Israel: _____
    c. Great Commission: _____
    d. Conversion of sinners: _____
    e. Security of saints:_____
    f. Destructiveness of ignorance: _____

3. What kind of heart should the teacher possess? _____
    _____

4. What effect is the Word of God to have on the life of a teacher?_____
    _____
    _____

5. Jesus grew in four areas. Discuss the importance of teachers growing in each of these areas:
    a. Spiritual:_____
    b. Mental:_____
    c. Social:_____
    d. Physical: _____

Lesson 3

Fundamentals of Successful Teaching (1)

I am only one, but still I am one; I cannot do everything, but still I can do something; and because I cannot do everything, I will not refuse to do something that I can do. – Edward E. Hale

The Power of Teachers

Teachers are powerful people. They have the power to advise and encourage. They can change and influence lives. Teachers possess this power as long as they keep trying to reach every student. The power of teaching can never be taken from a person; it can only be forfeited.

Teachers should never let anyone talk them out of being the best people and the best teachers they can be. They can and do influence students daily in significant ways. Bible class teachers help them discover spiritual interests while uncovering their strengths and talents. What is taught will be absorbed and you will make life better for your students. As a teacher you can alter lives permanently and eternally.

You will not always be able to see the results of your efforts. You will not always be able to judge accurately your effectiveness. There will be times when it appears that the students are unresponsive, only to find out years later that they were. A student who returns to thank you or just have a chat will put into perspective the power of teaching. Teachers need to be aware of the power they have.

To maintain this power, teachers need to consistently do three things:

1. Listen to, learn from, and respond to students.

2. Share the power of the classroom. Students need to have responsibilities in the classroom.

3. Continually try to teach and reach all students all of the time. Never give up on a student or surrender a moment of instructional time.

The effective teacher knows it takes a strong person to be a good teacher. It takes intelligence. It takes hard work. It takes resilience. But it also takes perspective and resolve. Without these attributes, we may give up our power.

Many important principles of successful teaching can be seen in Deuteronomy. 6:4-9:

Hear, O Israel! The Lord is our God, the Lord is one! And you shall love the Lord your God with all your heart, and with all your soul and with all your might. And these words, which I am commanding you this day, shall be on your heart; and you shall teach them diligently to your sons, and shall talk of them when you sit in your house, and when you walk by the way, and when you lie down, and when you rise up. And you shall bind them as a sign on your hand, and they shall be as frontals on your forehead. And you shall write them on the doorposts of your house, and on your gates.

As teachers we need not only to teach those in our care, but also to talk with them. With excitement and interest we need to communicate the knowledge which we possess. The students need to observe that we are interested in what we are teaching. The practical side of Bible knowledge needs to be communicated as we talk with them "by the way." Teachers need to take advantage of the little opportunities within and without the classroom to show how God's Word impacts a person's life. It may be a tussle in the church yard, a sad look on a face, or excitement about something new that will provide the teacher with an opportunity to "talk" as well as "teach."

All of our teaching is to be done with diligence. Diligence is not only a key to success as a student (2 Tim. 2:15), it is also a key to success as as teacher. Diligence in teaching requires that the lessons be well planned and delivered in an organized systematic manner. Teaching must be a high priority in one's life in order to ensure the sacrifice of hours of preparation.

Reinforcement and review are divinely ordained teaching methods. It is the unusual student who remembers everything he hears or reads the first time through. How many times have you, as an adult, read a familiar passage to find something new? You did not get it all the first time through. How much have you forgotten? Reinforcement and review are essential to making Bible knowledge a permanent part of our memory. Games, puzzles, and contests all help make review exciting and fun.

Teachers also need to have the proper attitude toward the inspiration of the Bible. We should not simply tell "Bible Stories" the way we might tell *Aesop's Fables.* Bible stories need to be presented as accurate historical accounts of real events. The person who does not have an unwavering, confident trust in the divine inspiration of the Bible does not need to be teaching until such time as those doubts are replaced with faith.

Prayer is an essential part of proper preparation and successful teaching. We should not attempt to bear the burden of teaching alone. Teachers need to request divine guidance and aid. Jesus frequently prayed before a teaching opportunity. If the Master Teacher needed to pray, how much more do you and I need the benefits of prayer?

A willingness to teach is also essential to successful teaching. The teacher must be willing to give unselfishly of himself in service to God. It is the willing and cheerful sacrifice that meets with the Lord's approval (2 Cor. 9:7). How effective can the teacher be who must be dragged, kicking and screaming, into the classroom?

Effective teachers express an excitement for the subject that they teach. We should be thrilled as we search the riches of God's Word. It is like a bottomless treasure chest always providing an exciting wealth of new spiritual prizes. To maximize effectiveness teachers need to make their room, voice, and presentation exciting and exhilarating.

Teachers need to be leaders not simply lecturers. The successful teacher strives to gain the maximum of class participation. Students of all ages enjoy being able to express themselves and ask questions. This makes students feel more a part of the class and makes them feel important.

The successful teacher is also a successful questioner. Questions set the pupil to thinking and working with the knowledge imparted. Such helps the student learn how to express themselves and their knowledge.

Proficient teachers use good illustrations. Verbal and visual illustrations are divinely authorized (see Matt. 22:17-22; Jer. 19). Illustrations help to clarify the subjects and enforce the lesson on the minds of the students. Stay alert to the things going on around you and you will discover a wealth of good illustrations. Think about the things which interest the students and the problems which they face and you will soon fill your treasure chest of illustrations. Good illustrations help make the lesson more interesting, practical, and meaningful.

Good teachers also show the practical application of the lesson. The Bible is the most practical book in the world and needs to presented as such. If a doctor gives his patient medicine but does not tell the patient how to use it, the patient will receive little benefit. Illustrations help fix the lesson on the mind, but applications fix it on their lives. Teachers need to tell the students "what's so" and then also tell them "so what."

Beatitudes for Bible Class Teachers

* *Blessed is* the teacher who has not sought the high places, but who has been

drafted into teaching because of his ability and willingness to teach.

- *Blessed is* the teacher who knows where he is going, why he is going, and how to get there.

- *Blessed is* the teacher who knows no discouragement, and who presents no alibi.

- *Blessed is* the teacher who knows to lead without being dictatorial; true leaders are humble individuals.

- *Blessed is* the teacher who seeks only the best for those whom he serves.

- *Blessed is* the teacher who teaches for the ultimate good of the most concerned, and not for the personal gratification and aggrandizement.

- *Blessed is* the teacher who develops teachers while teaching.

- *Blessed is* the teacher who marches with the group, and interprets correctly the signs on the pathway that leads to ultimate success.

- *Blessed is* the teacher who had his head in the clouds, feet on the ground, and is anchored in God's Word.

- *Blessed is* the teacher who considers teaching as an opportunity and service to the Lord and mankind.

Questions

1. From Deuteronomy 6:4-9, identify the following principles of effective teaching:
   a. Talking as well as teaching: _____
   b. Diligence: _____
   c. Reinforcement: _____
   d. Proper attitude toward Scriptures and Deity: _____
2. What is the difference between teaching and talking? _____
   _____
3. Why do we need to pray as we prepare to teach, before we teach, and after we have taught? _____
   _____
4. Discuss the importance of each of the following:
   a. Willingness to teach: _____
   b. Excitement about teaching: _____
   c. Good questions: _____
   d. Good illustrations: _____
   e. Making applications of the lesson: _____
5. Discuss the difference between teaching "what's so" and "so what." Why is each important? _____
   _____

6. Think of the best Bible class teacher you ever had. What were some of the characteristics and qualities which caused you to admire him? _____

    _____

    _____

    Why do you think he was an outstanding Bible teacher? _____

    _____

    _____

Lesson 4

Fundamentals of Successful Teaching (2)

Basic Principles of Learning

Involvement

Learning, like motivation, requires the active participation of the individual. Just as no one can motivate me (I must motivate myself), no one can learn for me. I must learn for myself. No one can force another person to remain mentally involved in a lesson. The student may appear to be bright eyed and listening while nearly comatose on the inside.

The effective Bible class teacher will create an atmosphere in which learning will be encouraged and enhanced. He will prepare materials and activities that will promote the active involvement of each student. Never lose sight of this one important principle: Teaching is not just dispensing information. It is the acquisition of information by the student. Learning takes place only when the learner is involved and an active participant in the process. You may lecture quite well. You may dole out some useful information, but unless the student is involved very little will be accomplished.

The teacher has a responsibility in the process of learning to see that involvement takes place. If the students are unmotivated or uninterested, the teacher should look to himself first. Has he given the students an opportunity to be involved or are they passive observers in the process? Have they been given the impression that they aren't really needed in this process? If nothing much about how the class was conducted or what went on in the class would be changed if the students were removed, then something is drastically wrong. Nothing motivates learning like learning!

Learning is self-perpetuating. I know of no greater motivator of learning or any greater reward for learning than the feeling of satisfaction and accomplishment that occurs when a person knows that he has learned something. Observe the excitement with which a young child bursts through the front door after everything has clicked and he knows he can read! At least for a while, it's hard to get him to stop. The same thing is true when it comes to Bible learning. As Bible class teachers, you can promote the enthusiastic learning of God's Word by helping the students know that they have learned. By asking good questions and encouraging them to "put things together," you can help them achieve the "Ah-hah" feeling. One key to successful teaching is feedback. The students need to know that they have learned, and the teacher needs to tell them so. Feedback will help the student and the teacher to make the needed adjustments. This needs to take place before the class begins as you wait on students to arrive, while you are walking out of class, and during class. Be constantly aware of where your students are!

Learning Occurs On Many Levels

People retain information in relation to how it is presented. There is an old Chinese Proverb which states:

> Tell me, I forget;
> Show me, I remember;
> Involve me, I understand.

The average person retains about 20% of what he hears, 30% of what he sees, and about 50% of what he sees and hears. However, he will retain about 90% of what he hears, sees, and does. Going beyond the seeing and hearing method of teaching requires more mental activity and a greater commitment on the part of the student.

Effective teachers direct their students into activities where the students have to do something with the information gained in the lesson. This can be accomplished through a variety of activities on many levels. The students can demonstrate something, write about something or someone, draw a picture, role-play a situation, investigate and analyze a case study, or defend a belief. Older students might put their knowledge of the responsibility to help others to work by getting together outside of class and raking leaves for an elderly couple. The possibilities are bounded only by the scope of your imagination. The key is to get the student involved beyond the hearing or seeing level. Teach to the students' level.

You cannot teach a two-year-old how to answer the liberal critics of the book of Daniel. You would not want to spend your class time having teenagers sing "This Little Light of Mine." The various emotional, physical, mental, and social levels of the students must be taken into consideration. I would encourage those who are interested in truly becoming great teachers to get a book describing these aspects of child development and become well acquainted with the level they desire to teach.

Beyond these considerations, the effective teacher will get to know his students on a personal basis. This will help him address the specific needs of his students. These activities may prove to be time consuming, but they will be helpful!

- Observe them in a different setting.
- Visit with them in their homes having them show you around their house. Have them share special possessions with you.
- Talk with their parents.
- Take advantage of the little opportunities before and after classes.
- Arrange social gatherings and outings for your class.
- Get to know your students and teach to their needs.
- Be Flexible!

The effective teacher will be flexible. If a teacher is not flexible, he will eventually break! There is no one best way to teach. There is not one best approach that will always work. What works with one class at one point in time will be a flop with another. You may have what you think is a great lesson prepared only to find out that it is too difficult or too easy. Be flexible. Bend, don't break. The effective teacher will make adjustments in his lesson content and approach depending on the circumstances.

Six Rules of Teaching

In addition to these considerations, let me briefly address a few other helpful suggestions.

1. Know what you are to teach before you go to class. There's no substitute for good preparation.

2. Know what changes you are seeking in your pupil's knowledge and behavior before you teach the lesson.

3. Gain and keep the attention of the pupil on the lesson. Help the students focus on the lesson and what you hope to accomplish.

4. Use words, illustrations, and methods that can be understood the same way by the students and teacher.

5. Lead the student from what he knows to what he does not know. Begin with the familiar and then help him explore the unknown (see the example of Jesus in Lk. 24:44-48).

6. Repeat, review, and reproduce the lesson. None of us retains everything he learns the first time that he is exposed to it. Repetition is an effective teacher. Weekly review is essential to the long term retention of knowledge.

The effective teacher will acquire a knowledge of how students learn. While the learning process is not as important as the eternal truths imparted, an awareness of it will make the teaching more effective and the results more long lasting.

Questions

1. What are some physical things in the classroom which might affect the student's learning? _____

   _____

   _____

2. Describe what you would consider to be the ideal learning atmosphere. ___

   _____

   _____

3. Tell how you think a teacher might improve each of these situations:

   a. The teacher does most of the talking._____

   _____

   b. The teacher reads from the workbook and appears to be "tied" to it. __

   _____

   c. Covering the content of the lesson is of upmost importance. _____

   _____

   d. A busy life leaves only a short time on Sunday mornings to prepare for class._____

   _____

4. What important principle of teaching can be gleaned from 1 Corinthians 14:9? _____

   _____

5. Read the following passage and evaluate the teaching techniques used: Luke 24:44-48; John 4:1-42. _____

   _____

   _____

Lesson 5

Questioning Techniques For Bible Class Teachers (1)

- "For what does it profit a man to gain the whole world and forfeit his soul?" (Matt. 16:26).

- "And why do you look at the speck in your brother's eye, but do not notice the log that is in your own eye?" (Matt. 7:3).

- "Who do people say that I am?" (Matt. 16:13).

Throughout His ministry, Jesus often asked questions of His audience. He was not only the "Master Teacher," He was the "Master Questioner." He recognized the value of asking good questions and used them often as a valuable teaching tool. If we are to be effective Bible teachers today, we must recognize the value of good questions and use them properly.

The Master's Use of Questions

Jesus used questions to accomplish a number of important tasks:

1. He frequently asked questions as He taught to *arouse the interest of his audience.* These questions were not always difficult to answer. In fact, they were quite often simple questions which did little more than get the audience thinking. For instance, in Matthew 5:13, ". . .if the salt has become tasteless, how will it be made salty again?" His audience knew the answer and their response did not require great mental activity. Later in Matthew 6:27 he asked, "And which of you by being anxious can add a single cubit to his life's span?" By asking these questions Jesus provoked the audience to think about what He was discussing. Such prompted the audience to become a mental participant of the discussion.

2. He asked questions to *get a commitment from the audience.* Jesus often asked very pointed questions that required the audience to declare their commitment or lack of it. He asked a group of blind men in Matthew 9:28, "Do you believe that I am able to do this?" He questioned His disciples, "But who do you say that I am?" (Matt. 16:15). The audience had to make a careful self-inspection

and whether or not they verbalized the answer, declare a commitment or lack of it to what was being discussed.

3. On occasion He *would answer a question with a question* leading the audience to find their own answer. When asked by the Pharisees why His disciples transgressed the commandments of God, He responded, "And why do you yourselves transgress the commandment of God for the sake of your tradition?" (Matt. 15:1-3). He challenged the chief priests when they protested the adoration directed toward Jesus by asking, ". . .have you never read, 'out of the mouths of infants and nursing babes thou hast prepared praise for Thyself'?" (Matt. 21:15-16). By doing this He required that the individual think for himself and search his mind for the answer. The questions were so pointed that only one conclusion could be rightly drawn.

Jesus Used Questions To
- Arouse the interest of His audience
- Gain a commitment from His audience
- Answer another question
- Test the understanding of the audience
- Get the audience to inspect themselves
- Provoke the audience to deeper thought
- Confound His enemies

4. He asked questions to *test the understanding* of the audience. The teacher needs to know whether or not the audience is understanding what is being taught. Jesus frequently asked questions such as, "Have you understood all these things?" (Matt. 13:51) or "Do you not yet understand or remember the five loaves of the five thousand. . .?" (Matt. 16:9). Such questions aided the teacher and the student by ensuring a proper understanding and application of the lessons being taught.

5. He asked questions designed to cause the audience to *inspect themselves.* He confronted His sleeping disciples in the garden and asked, "So, you could not keep watch with Me for one hour?" (Matt. 26:40) He challenged the faith of the same men when He came to them on the water and asked, "O you of little faith, why did you doubt?" (Matt. 14:31). For the most part these questions were not designed to be answered orally, but were simply given as thought questions. What Jesus taught would have been of little value if it had not been applied personally. The audience needed to measure themselves according to the standard being advanced by Jesus.

6. Jesus asked questions to provoke the audience to *deeper thought.* He aroused the interest of Peter and caused him to think more deeply when they were confronted by the tax collectors in Capernaum (Matt. 17:24-27). Rather than brow-beating Peter for his impetuous response to the tax collectors' question, Jesus invited him to ponder this situation by asking him a question. Jesus

asked, "From whom do the kings of the earth collect customs or poll-tax, from their sons or from strangers?" By asking this question, Peter was caused to ponder the relationship between Christ and the Father, for whose service the tax was being collected. The question was an easy one, but the implications far reaching. Jesus was always interested in His audience gaining a deep under-standing of His lesson and used good questions to provoke them to consider and meditate upon His teaching.

7. Also in a most masterful way, Jesus used questions to *confound his en-emies.* Like Nathan, Jesus used questions to get His audience to accuse and judge themselves. He unveiled the evil and hypocritical motives of His enemies by asking questions which confounded and exposed them. When asked about paying taxes to Caesar He asked for a coin and said, "Whose likeness and inscrip-tion is this?" (Matt. 22:20). The chief priests and elders sought to entrap Jesus on another occasion by questioning His authority. He responded with a question of His own, "The baptism of John was from what source, from heaven or from men?" (Matt. 21:25). He stopped the mouths of His enemies and caused them to see, whether or not they admitted it to themselves, the truth.

Conclusion

Jesus the "Master Teacher" was also the "Master Questioner." He knew when and how to ask good questions. He did not monopolize the air space in every teaching situation. He sought to involve His students mentally and stimulate them to greater thought and understanding. Wanting them to make personal application of His truths, He questioned their understanding and depth of knowledge. As teachers we would do well to take a lesson from the Master and sharpen our questioning skills.

In a survey of adult Bible class students, it was found that the majority de-scribed their favorite teachers as the ones who lead a class discussion with the use of good questions. According to those who responded the questions served the following purposes:

- Aroused and kept the interest of the audience.
- Provided for greater class participation.
- Caused the audience to think more deeply.
- Made each class member feel important in the class process.

Your classes can become more interesting, stimulating, and productive by mastering the art of asking good questions.

Questions

1. Find an example, other than those used in this text, of Jesus asking questions for each of the following purposes.
   a. Arousing the interest of the audience: _____
   b. Gaining a commitment from the audience: _____
   c. Answering another question: _____
   d. Testing the understanding of the audience: _____
   e. Getting audience to inspect themselves: _____
   f. Provoking deeper thought: _____
   g. Confounding enemies: _____
2. Choose a story about a well known Old Testament character and develop questions which will. . .
   a. Arouse the interest of your students when you introduce the story._____
      _____
   b. Test their understanding of the basic facts of the story._____
      _____
   c. Provoke them to deeper thought about the needed application from the story. _____
      _____
   d. Cause the students to inspect themselves._____
      _____

Lesson 6

Questioning Techniques
For Bible Class Teachers (2)

He that gives good advice, builds with one hand;
He that gives good counsel and example, builds with both.

- Francis Bacon

Guidelines for Asking Good Questions

Asking questions will cause the students to think. After all, isn't this the object of all teaching? Little good will be accomplished if the students do not engage in some mental gymnastics. Always keep this goal in mind when asking questions and responding to answers.

Ask questions that will encourage the students to express what they have learned. We do not teach simply to educate the student, but also to prepare him to teach others. "And the things which you have heard from me in the presence of many witnesses, these entrust to faithful men, who will be able to teach others also" (2 Tim. 2:2). If our students are to mature in knowledge and skill so that they can teach others, we must help them learn how to express the knowledge that they have. Not only will this help fix the lesson on their minds, it will help the teacher evaluate the effectiveness of his instruction.

Posture your queries in pellucid, facile, and fathomable terms. Make sense? Need a dictionary? Frustrating? I don't blame you. More simply put, it is always best to ask your questions in clear, simple, and easily understood terms. If your students do not understand the question, they can neither answer nor gain from the question.

Allow the students a chance to think before answering the question. To allow students time to think before answering requires patience on the part of the teacher. The moments of silent thought may seem like a long time, but they will be golden. A few moments of silence does not indicate time wasted. On the contrary, it may be some of your most productive time. It does little good if an impatient teacher asks and quickly answers the questions himself.

Ask questions that are applicable to the lesson under consideration. This will help keep the class on track. Once a teacher has begun to master the art of asking good questions and the students have begun to feel comfortable in responding, you may find the discussion going far afield. While it may occasionally be profitable to allow the discussion to wander, the limited amount of time allotted to Bible instruction makes it imperative that you stay on track. Good questions that help to lead and corral an enthusiastic discussion will make a positive contribution to effective Bible instruction.

It is helpful to word your questions in such a way that they demand multi-word answers. When you simply want to test the students' recall of basic facts, questions requiring only one word answers will be appropriate. But, when you are wanting to determine their grasp of basic concepts and applications, you need to ask questions that will provoke a great deal of thinking and class input.

Types of Questions

On occasion you will want to ask questions just to test the facts presented in a lesson. In asking such questions, it will be helpful to keep the following in mind:

1. Some facts are important in and of themselves. Some are interesting to recall because of their uniqueness.

2. Some facts are worth remembering because of their cultural value.

3. Some facts are important building blocks for future generalizations and principles. These facts are the ones most important to the Bible class teacher. The student will need certain basic information to gain the important spiritual applications contained in the lessons.

Questions requiring a recall of facts should be simply stated and easily understood.

Additionally, you will want to ask questions for the purpose of generating class discussion. In asking such questions keep in mind:

1. Word the questions so as to require more than a one or two word answer. A discussion consisting of one or two word answers is not particularly stimulating.

2. Word the questions so as to make it possible for the correct response to be worded in a number of ways.

3. Allow plenty of time for the students to think about their answer. Allow the required amount of silence. They cannot think and listen to you at the same time. Something will have to give.

4. Compliment and encourage each respondent. Nothing will inspire conversation and stimulate discussion like a few appropriate compliments. If you are

harshly critical of the students or pick apart every answer they give, they will soon tire of risking a critique. As much as possible try to be positive in your response. Even if the student is wrong, you can compliment his willingness to respond.

5. After one response, when appropriate, encourage others to attempt to answer the question in their own words. Someone else in the class may word a response in just enough of a different way to add much to the learning process.

Level of Questions
"Recall Questions"

As we have stated, many questions simply require that the students recall some basic facts. Such questions are beneficial and should be part of each class discussion. However, these questions do not require much mental activity. These questions should be used, but not exclusively. The good questioner will not limit his questions to this level.

Key words to use in asking "Recall Questions."

Tell	What	Show
Describe	Who	Which
Recall	Define	Identify
Make a list	Name	When

Examples of "Recall Questions" (from Acts 16)
*   Where did Paul go after Neapolis?
*   Whom did Paul meet by the river?
*   What was the product which Lydia sold?
*   Name the man thrown into prison with Paul.

"Translation Questions":

Some questions require that the student translate information. This requires that the students do more than simply recall information. The student must change the information into a new form by establishing relationships, principles, and generalizations. Such requires a higher level of thinking.

Key words to use in asking "Translation Questions."

Characterize	Associate	Give an example
Compare	In your own words	Rephrase
Contrast	Explain	Which

Examples of "Translation Questions":
*   Compare Lydia's reaction to the Gospel to that of the Jailor's.
*   In your own words, tell why Paul and Silas were thrown in jail.
*   Give an example of where purple fabric was used for something special.
*   How would you characterize Lydia's attitude toward spiritual matters?

"Application Questions":

Some questions require that the student make an application of what they have learned. In such questions the student is often required to solve some real life problem by using his new knowledge. These are more difficult than the previous two types of questions and thus demand more mental activity.

Key words to use in asking "Application Questions."

Apply	In this case	Consider
How would	Solve	Tell us how

Examples of "Application Questions"

- How might an application of Paul's attitude upon hearing the "Macedonian call" cause the church to grow more rapidly today?
- How can the cases of Lydia and the Jailor be used today to show the importance of baptism?
- Consider and tell us how you might be able to use the gospel to help someone with a great and pressing personal problem.
- What should Paul and Silas' attitude while in jail tell us today?

"Analyzing and Synthesizing Questions":

Some questions require that the student analyze and then synthesize the information which he has gained. This requires higher levels of thinking, but can be effectively used with most levels. Such requires that the student solve a problem with creative thought using and bringing together all available material. The student must categorize information and determine which is most useful.

Some key words to use in asking "Analyzing and Synthesizing Questions."

Why	Distinguish	Summarize
Imagine	Describe	Conclude
Analyze	Think of a way	Classify

Examples of "Analyzing and Synthesizing Questions"

- Why would Phillipi have been a good place for Paul to preach and establish a church?
- Summarize the various responses given Paul by those whom he contacted in Acts 16.
- Classify those whom Paul contacted in Acts 16 as either sincere, indifferent, or hostile.
- Why did Paul become annoyed by the spirit in the young girl?

"Evaluation Questions":

The last category of questions involve the skills of evaluation. These require the student to use all available information and make certain judgments based upon that information. This involves the highest level of thinking skills.

Some key words to use in asking "Evaluation Questions."

Evaluate	What would . . . have done
Decide	What is most important. . .
Judge	What is most appropriate. . .
Defend	Choose

Examples of "Evaluation Questions"

- What was the most important attitude possessed by the Jailor and Lydia? In times of crisis, what are some appropriate actions?
- Was Paul right or wrong in being annoyed with the spirit of the young girl?
- How might things have turned out differently had Paul and Silas not have been imprisoned?

Conclusion

A variety of types of questions needs to be used in each lesson. When only one type of question is used, the class has the potential of becoming boring, frustrating, discouraging, or unstimulating. A good mix of questions will contribute to an effective learning atmosphere. It is often beneficial to begin with the lower level questions and build to the more difficult and challenging.

As much as possible have your questions written out ahead of time. This will allow you the time to review and refine your questions. Yet you will need to be flexible enough to ask follow up questions. Your best question stimulators will often be the students themselves. When responding and following up, don't be afraid to "play the devil's advocate." You can stimulate a lot of higher level thinking by arguing with the students and having them defend their views.

You may find it helpful to arrange your classroom to reflect a discussion arrangement. Circles, semi-circles, and table arrangements will be more likely to stimulate discussion than straight rows where students stare at the backs of one another's heads. In addition, you need to be "on their level." Sit with them. Don't posture yourself as being aloof.

Questions

Choose one of the following texts and prepare five questions from each of the five levels of questions.

Matthew 5	**Acts 2**	**Romans 12:8-2**
Matthew 27	**Acts 8**	**Hebrews 11**

1. Recall questions:

_____

_____

_____

_____

_____

2. Translation questions:

_____

_____

_____

_____

_____

3. Application questions:

_____

_____

_____

_____

_____

4. Analyzing and synthesizing questions:

_____

_____

_____

_____

_____

5. Evaluation questions:

_____

_____

_____

_____

_____

Lesson 7

Discipline in the Bible Class (1)

Don't find fault.
Find a remedy.
– Henry Ford

Problems Will Occur!

No one, including the students, enjoys a disruptive class room. I suppose that every teacher and every student have at one time or another felt as if their very last nerve was about to be stomped on by a disruptive student. This is not a pleasant situation. The teacher cannot teach and the students cannot learn when they are being vexed by disruptions.

Every teacher has had his encounters with a discipline problem (if he claims to have never had a problem with any student he is probably either lying or is terribly blind to the situation in his classroom!). You are not alone. You have not failed as a teacher when disruptions occur. When facing discipline problems in a classroom, don't give up! Hang in there, make adjustments, seek help, and you'll be fine.

What Is Discipline?

Discipline is far more than simply punishing a student when he misbehaves or dealing with some undesirable action on the part of the student. Discipline comes from the same root word as "disciple." It refers to a process of learning, training, and growing. It is a systematic method of training, molding, correcting, or perfecting the intellect and moral character of an individual.

Discipline is the process of helping an individual learn self-control. When we discipline, we establish boundaries within which the students are expected to operate. As the student grows in self-control, we establish fewer boundaries for them because they are able to create their own. It is the teacher's responsibility to enforce boundaries of behavior fairly and consistently so the student may learn what is acceptable behavior and what is not.

Instructive discipline is preventative in nature. It seeks to prevent problems before they arise. Instructive discipline will provide the students with boundaries and expectations. Paul provided the Ephesians with instructive discipline when he did not shrink from declaring to them anything that was profitable, having declared to them the whole purpose of God (Acts 20:20, 27). Bible class teachers have an obligation to instruct students in the ways of the Lord, instructing them regarding their duties, responsibilities, and obligations before God. It will also involve pointing out areas of short comings, sometimes coupled with warnings and admonitions.

Punitive discipline is corrective in nature. When instructive discipline alone is not effective it becomes necessary to use punitive discipline. As with instructive discipline, punitive discipline is designed to save souls. Punitive discipline is not pleasant to receive or dispense. No punishment will seem to be joyful to either the student or teacher; however, it must be remembered that "all discipline for the moment seems not to be joyful, but sorrowful; yet to those who have been trained by it, afterwards it yields the peaceful fruit of righteousness" (Heb. 12:11).

Necessity of Discipline

If you have ever been in a classroom where no boundaries have been drawn or enforced, you understand the necessity of discipline. In the midst of this sea of confusion, no learning can take place. If the students are not learning, then the class has become a waste of time.

There needs to be an air of "specialness" to Bible class time. The students have assembled to learn about God, His Word, and His expectations of them. This requires reverent and respectful behavior. This is a special time and place which the students need to learn to respect. Behavior that might be acceptable on a playground or during free time at home may not be appropriate for this special time and place. Students have come to learn not to play. They need to learn this and teachers need to model and teach it.

Further, God demands that when people assemble to worship Him they do all things decently and in order (1 Cor. 14:40). This includes Bible class time.

The time allotted by most congregations for Bible study is extremely short. In most congregations, there is at the most two hours of organized Bible study a week. Sadly, for many students this is the only Bible study they will receive for the week. This time is short and precious. There is not a moment to waste. When disorder reigns supreme, there is no learning taking place, and time is wasted. With such a short time allotted, can we afford to allow disruptions to rob the students of these precious few moments?

Parents will appreciate a well disciplined classroom. The corralling of the students' energies and enthusiasm by appropriate boundaries will have an important carry-over into the remainder of the worship. You can watch the students as they file into the auditorium and generally tell which have come from classes where the teacher exercised appropriate discipline and which did not. Parents will not only appreciate the knowledge that their children have acquired, they will also treasure the respectful behavior that is being learned.

Students will also appreciate a well disciplined classroom. Although they will often be slow to admit it, students like to learn in orderly environments. They like to know what the limits are and to have them fairly enforced.

Your success as a Bible class teacher will, to a large extent, depend on how successful you are in maintaining discipline and order in your classroom. If you want to leave each session with a feeling of satisfaction and accomplishment, then good discipline is a necessity. You're not being mean, you're being a teacher!

Could The Teacher Be The Problem?

One of the first places that a teacher should look when his classroom becomes disruptive is in the mirror. Sadly, one of the most common causes of disruption is the teacher. It will do little good for the teacher to instruct or punish students if he is a major cause of the problem. Teachers can contribute to disruption in a variety of ways:

• *By not being properly prepared.* This may leave the lesson dry and uninteresting. The students will then seek out other things to occupy their minds. The teacher may not have enough planned for the class period and thus leave the students with time for mischief.

• *By not arriving on time.* The teacher should be the first person in the room. This will allow the teacher time to greet each student, show interest in each one, and limit the pre-class activities. If the students have been running wild before the teacher arrives, the teacher will face a tremendous task in attempting to regain control and corral the excitement.

• *By not taking a personal interest in each student.* If a student does not get positive, personal attention from the teacher, he is likely to find ways to simply get attention. When the students have a positive feeling about themselves, the class, and the teacher, they are far more likely to be cooperative. Personal attention and interest will help accomplish this end.

• *Telling the students that they are bad or mean.* If a teacher constantly tells a student that they are bad, mean, or a problem, they will most likely live out that expectation. There are no "bad kids." There are plenty who engage in bad deeds, but I object to calling them "bad kids."

• *By not being flexible.* Have you ever had a day when you had difficulty paying attention at work or at home? Have you ever just not felt like doing much? Well, students have the same kind of days. Have you ever had a problem that just wouldn't wait? Students also have those kinds of problems and need to talk about them *now*. The effective teacher must be flexible enough to allow for these kinds of situations. Sometimes a joke or a little levity can help defuse a potentially disruptive situation and give the students the breather they need. Teachers need to be flexible and able to adapt to every changing situation in their classroom.

• *By failing to show interest and excitement in the lessons. If* you're not interested and excited, how can you expect the students to be? Mrs. Bessie Mae Cox was the best teacher I had during my public school education. She was strict and could swing a mean paddle. But, she always began each day with a smile and a funny little bounce in her step as she began each lesson. Her enthusiasm was contagious. Interested and motivated students will be cooperative students.

• *By failing to speak so as to be understood.* If the students cannot understand the words that you use, you cannot expect to keep their attention. If you "talk down" to them, they will be insulted and more prone to disruption.

Other Causes of Disruption

Another frequent cause of disruption is the classroom itself. If the room is crowded, cluttered, dirty, or "sterile," it may contribute to the problem. Seating arrangements can encourage too much talking or can encourage fidgeting and poking. A room that is too cold or too hot will cause student's to be uncomfortable and irritable (not to mention a cranky teacher). Outside noise also affects the behavior of the class as it can make concentration more difficult.

Sometimes the student's home life is a contributor to the problem. If the students are not made to behave at home, it will be difficult to get them to behave in Bible class. If the students get little or no attention at home, they may come to Bible class starved for attention and willing to do anything to get attention. Many situations at home that carry over into the Bible class are temporary and simply have to be endured. Others need and must receive attention. The influence of the home cannot and should not be ignored. The teacher can contribute positively to a disciplined environment in his classroom by getting to know what's going on at home. Teachers should be encouraged to visit students in their homes, get to know the parents, and the situations the children face at home. This will help the teacher to be more sympathetic and will foster cooperation between the parents and the teacher.

Questions

1. Define discipline: _____
    _____

2. Find Bible examples of the two types of discipline and discuss the necessity
    of each. _____
    _____

3. What is the goal of classroom discipline? _____
    _____

4. Why is discipline necessary in the classroom? _____
    _____

5. How can each of the following contribute to discipline problems in the class-
    room?
    a. The teacher:_____
        _____

    b. The classroom:_____
        _____

    c. The home: _____
        _____

Lesson 8

Discipline in the Classroom (2)

No amount of instructive or preventative discipline will eliminate every discipline problem. Don't be surprised when problems occur; simply be ready for them with a plan of action.

Considerations in Exercising Discipline

Discipline must be fair, firm, friendly, and consistent. If any of these is violated, the discipline will not be effective and the teacher's conduct may lead to even more severe problems. A teacher who is not fair may cause the students to become bitter, disrespectful, and even more disruptive. Discipline must be firm. If the students perceive that the teacher is lacking in resolve, they will often test the situation to see how much farther they can go. If the teacher becomes angry or mean when disciplining students, whatever is done will most likely backfire. Sarcasm or harshness should never be used in correcting a student. This is likely to make the student bitter and will cause the teacher more severe problems later. Inconsistent discipline will cause further confusion and disruption. Never threaten to do something that you are not willing to do. If the students chooses to call your bluff and you loose, your credibility is shot.

Remember to reward positive behavior as well as punishing inappropriate behavior. The cooperative students need to know that they are appreciated and have their behavior reinforced. This will set a positive example for the rest of the class. The student who misbehaves in order to receive attention will learn that there are other ways to gain the attention of his teacher. The disruptive student needs to know when he has been good. A smile, hug, note of approval, or pat on the back can help establish a positive atmosphere where disruptions occur less frequently. In addition, these positive episodes need to be shared with the parents. Every parent likes to hear that his child has accomplished something worthy of praise. Communicating positive behaviors and accomplishments will also help ensure cooperation between the teacher and parents.

Never forget that you are the teacher and you are in charge. As the adult in the room, assert your authority and determine that no child will totally disrupt your class. Don't be afraid to let the students know that you are in charge. Communicate your authority in a kind way and conduct yourself so as to be worthy of their respect. Your time is too limited and the Word of God too precious to allow a disruptive student to cheat others of their opportunity to learn.

What works with one student will not necessarily work with another student. What one teacher finds effective in one class may bomb in your class. The likes and dislikes of each group will differ. Be flexible enough to adapt to the situation in which you find yourself. Don't become rigid in your classroom management. Remember the teacher who will not bend will eventually break!

Set definite, easily understood rules to govern classroom behavior. Make sure that your students understand these rules. With younger students you will need more rules, and these rules will need to be more specific. But as the students get older, the rules need to become more general. This will help direct the students in a quest for self-control. For example, with a group of lower elementary students, you might determine that students should remain in their seats and not write on the table. However, with high school students, you might simply say that they are to show respect for their physical surroundings. If you have a mature group of students, you might want to have them make suggestions as to what rules should be established. Rules and expectations should address respect for God, the teacher, fellow students, and the classroom.

Not everything that you find irritating needs to receive your attention. Teachers need to learn how to ignore some behaviors, even though they are bothersome. Several years ago I taught a class of lower elementary students. In this class I had a little boy who had great difficulty sitting in his seat the "correct way." He wiggled and twisted like a rock star. I was convinced that he wasn't listening to a thing I had to say. Yet when review questions were asked, he was able to give the correct answer to each question. I found it irritating, but it did not bother the other students or the boy. A particular behavior is not a problem until it has gotten the attention of others and interfered with the learning process.

Always try to defuse the situation with as little action and as few of words as possible. Often a chatty student can be quieted by simply moving in his direction. A hand or squeeze on his shoulder will often be all that is necessary to get the message across. If you are sitting at a table with the students, try standing up for a while. This will establish your physical presence and may quietly regain the attention of those who are disruptive. A moment of silence can be an effective tool in regaining the attention of the class.

If these "quiet" things do not help, try moving the student to another seat or corner away from everyone else. I know of one teacher who keeps a "naughty chair" in her classroom. This is reserved for extraordinary occasions when students refuse to cooperate.

Don't allow discipline problems to drag on. Most will only get worse with time. What might be easily solved if addressed quickly, can become a major disruption when allowed time to ferment. If the students perceive that you have lost control, they will lose respect for you.

Toys, new purses, pencils, or other items that cause disruptions can be quietly taken away. I am convinced that, with young students, these things should not be allowed in the classroom. The students can have "show-n-tell" outside of class. If these items are not brought in, they can't cause problems.

Developing a Discipline Plan

Proper preparation and preventative discipline will eliminate most potential classroom disruptions. However, regardless of what you as the teacher do, there will be occasions when punitive discipline needs to take place. For the benefit of the students, this needs to be carefully developed and understood by parents and students.

Don't lose sight of the purpose of punitive discipline. The purpose of punitive discipline is to correct the behavior of the offending student, not satisfy your ego, release your tension, or seek revenge.

Just as the effective teacher will have the classroom rules developed before the class begins, he will also have a "plan of action" for disciplinary problems in place before entering the classroom. This discipline plan needs to be understood by the students and their parents. Any such plan should be developed in cooperation with the local elders to ensure their approval and backing.

A Suggested Plan

1. Notify the class during the first session of what is expected of them concerning behavior, preparation, etc.

2. Determine if this situation deserves attention or would be better ignored. If attention is deserved begin by using the least invasive method available.

3. Speak quietly and privately with the disruptive student, making sure that he understands what behavior was offensive. It may be helpful to have him repeat the rule that was broken and how he broke it. Focus on the behavior not the student.

4. If the misbehavior continues during the class period, give the student a second warning. Be firm in your correction. Depending on the situation and the child, you may need to do this in front of the entire class.

5. If the misbehavior continues in that or subsequent class periods, try removing the student from the classroom or sit them in a "time-out" chair separated from his classmates. Be sure to notify the parents that this action was necessary. Allow the student to return at the next class session.

6. If the student continues to disrupt the class then you may need to remove him from the class, sitting him with his parents until such time as it is determined that he will cooperate. This may seem severe, but you cannot allow one student to prevent others from learning.

Conclusion

Discipline must take into account the four relationships that exist in every classroom.

1. Student and Self. The effective teacher will look at how students view themselves. Do they think that they are important, wanted, needed, intelligent, etc.? It is not so important how the teacher views the student. What is most important is how the student views himself.

2. Student and Peers. Students need to be accepted and feel like they are a part of a group. Peer rejection can be one cause of discipline problems. Effective teachers will help students fit in and belong.

3. Students and Class Activities. Some students may feel overwhelmed while others are bored and unchallenged. Each of these groups is a potential discipline problems.

4. Student and Teacher. The lack of a positive relationship between student and teacher often leads to discipline problems. Successful teachers try to establish and maintain a cordial, friendly relationship with students without losing respect by seeming like one of the gang.

Questions

1. Discuss the need for discipline to be fair, friendly, firm, and consistent. _____
    _____
    _____

2. Why is it important to individualize discipline? _____
    _____

3. Why is it important to ignore some behaviors? _____
    _____

    Give some examples of behaviors that you might find irritating, but that would be better ignored. _____
    _____
    _____

4. Give examples of how to quietly defuse a situation._____
    _____

5. Choose an age group and develop a set of appropriate rules. _____
    _____

6. Develop a suggested discipline plan for a particular age group._____
    _____

Games, Puzzles, and Other Activities

Learning is often more fun and exciting if it can be approached as a game. Such is not intended to minimize the importance of learning, or the sanctity of the Word of God. It is much easier to excite students of all ages about studying the Bible when they come to enjoy it. It will prove easier to gain and maintain the attention of students if they are having fun learning. It has been suggested that the optimum learning environment is one where the students do not know they are learning. After all, even cleaning the garage can be fun, if it is approached as a game. Puzzles, games, and similar activities can motivate students to challenge themselves and push themselves to greater depths of knowledge.

Biblical Precedent

Great teachers in the Bible did not confine themselves to the lecture or workbook method of teaching. Riddles, visual aids, and teaching aids were a part of their teaching. Consider just a few examples:

1. Jesus frequently used parables to teach deep spiritual lessons. This same method was utilized quite skillfully by Nathan when he found it necessary to confront David (2 Sam. 12:1-7).

2. Jesus used a coin to teach a lesson. Rather than just give the answer to the crowd, He chose to use a more creative and impacting method of teaching. His use of this visual aid is similar to today's teacher using a map, video, or other aid.

3. Jeremiah and Ezekiel were masters of illustration through the use of visual aids (see Jer. 19 or Ezek. 3).

Suggestions for Visual Aids

The following suggestions originated with Leonard Meuse of Polaroid.

1. Make only one point on a visual aid. The purpose of the visual is to focus attention on the main point.

2. Don't leave a visual aid on the screen too long. It will become distracting.

3. Keep them simple.

4. Make the main idea stand out and easily recognized.

5. When using a series of charts, keep them in the same style and look.

6. The visual must aid in understanding. A good visual will be understood in less than 15 seconds.

7. Address the topic at hand; don't allow the visuals to become a distraction.

8. Quality is important.

Games and Learning Activities

Games, riddles, puzzles, visual aids, and such like make learning more fun. We all know that what we enjoy we are more willing to do and will do better. These types of teaching methods should never be viewed as entertainment, but as tools of the master teacher.

Learning games and similar activities will encourage participation and involvement. Hopefully you will recall that these are keys to learning. When the students are kept mentally involved in the lesson, they will learn more. The more they have to think, scratch, and ponder, the more long lasting the lesson will be.

Simple games and learning activities can be inexpensively prepared by the teacher often with a minimum of effort. For those teachers who are not confident in their ability to make their own learning activities, many are available from reputable publishers. (Any time you use a commercially prepared puzzle, game, etc. be sure that you have checked it for scriptural accuracy.)

Any activity chosen should be checked for it appropriateness. The following checklist may prove helpful:

1. Does it teach a Bible principle or story? Does it reinforce the lesson? Just because it occupies the students' time or is fun doesn't mean that it is a profitable use of time. Make sure that the activity will actually enhance your teaching.

2. Some kinds of activities will teach a lesson, but will take up too much time. Your time to teach is limited, so make sure that the time allotted for the activity can be justified.

3. Is the activity appropriate for the age of the students? If the activity is too easy, the students will be bored. If it is too difficult, they will be frustrated. Know your students and their abilities. Gear the activities to their ability.

4. Will the students enjoy the activity? If the students are not enjoying what they are doing, then the activity has not met one of its stated goals.

5. Will participation in the activity embarrass any of the students? Most students enjoy competitive activities such as "Bible Quiz Bowls." But, some stu-

dents are so shy or insecure that participation can be very stressful. Again, know your students and adapt to their needs and personalities.

Suggested Activities

When making your own puzzles or activities, there are a few things to keep in mind:

1. Gear the difficulty of the puzzle to the age group being targeted.

2. Check the puzzle carefully for mistakes. A flawed puzzle is frustrating.

3. The words, concepts, and clues in the puzzle should be the key words from the lesson.

Make the clues easy to understand. Just because it's difficult doesn't mean that it is a good puzzle. The students must be able to read and understand your clues.

Crossword Puzzles

Crossword puzzles present a fun and effective way of getting the students to read the Bible text more closely or review previous lessons. They can be completed individually, in groups, or even by the whole class when presented on an overhead. Crossword Puzzles are reasonably simple to make and can be easily copied. A pad of light blue graph paper, ruler, and pencil are the only things you will need when making your own. I suggest light blue graph paper because that color will not be picked up by most copiers.

Seek-N-Find Puzzles

Seek-n-find puzzles are a favorite of upper elementary and junior high students. These are simple to make if you take time to map out the word flow carefully. Words can be scrambled by going up, down, diagonally, as well as backwards. The number of extra letters determines the difficulty, so keep that in mind when working with younger children. When making seek-n-find puzzles for older students, I like to include the answers almost spelled correctly to add to the difficulty. This way the student spends more time thinking about the words. Another way to make these even more effective is to give clues or ask questions rather than simply giving them a list of words to find. Graph paper, ruler, and pencil are the only tools you will need to make your own.

Riddles

Riddles present a clever and creative way of encouraging Bible reading and thinking. The object is to give just enough information for the student to ponder so he can then arrive at the answer. Good riddles are neither too difficult nor too easy. Remember your audience when preparing riddles. The examples below are rhyming riddles, but such would not have to be the case.

>   Was the water cold
>   So it made people shiver

When he baptized them
In the Jordan River?

He was the disciple
That, though he grieved,
In the Lord's resurrection
He hadn't yet believed?

That's Nonsense!

We are all familiar with the traditional true/false questions. These can be an effective tool for the teacher to use when trying to evaluate the students' learning. But, why not try a new twist? Give the students a group of statements all of which are false and have them correct the statement so that it is true rather than false. These types of questions can be easily incorporated into a game and used with all age groups. I find that, when made somewhat difficult, even adults enjoy them.

Bible Baseball

This game can be played with a minimum of preparation and is an exciting way to review. All you need are some questions and a baseball diamond drawn on the blackboard or taped off on the floor. The teacher is the "pitcher" who throws questions to the students who have been divided into two teams. If the student gets the answer correct, then he advances one base. If he misses it, then it counts as an out. When one team gets three outs, the other team gets to "bat."

Baseball is not the only sport which can be adapted to Bible teaching and review. A similar game can be played with football rules. Teams can draw questions from a bag with each question worth certain "yardage." One team can continue answering questions and advancing the ball until they either score or miss 4 questions. Other rules can be incorporated as appropriate.

TV Game Shows

There are a number of popular TV Game Shows which could be adapted for use by the creative Bible class teacher. Jeopardy is one such game. On a piece of cardboard construct the question board by using envelopes cut in half. Label the envelopes, in any number of columns, with certain values (10, 20, 30. . .). Each column can be given a special designation such as NAMES, NUMBERS, PLACES. . . . This game can be played with teams or individually. This is a great way to review specific lessons or general Bible knowledge. If you have difficulty finding enough questions, consult a Bible Trivia game.

"Password" and "Wheel of Fortune" are other popular game shows that easily lend themselves to Bible class instruction and review. Students enjoy the competition and challenge of these games. They will learn many important facts without realizing that they are learning!

The Question Train

This game requires quite a bit of preparation and creativity, but when done properly can last for years and challenge even the most gifted students. Construct a train with an engine, caboose, and one boxcar for each letter of the alphabet. Glue envelopes or something to hold questions on the box cars. The answers to each question in a particular boxcar should all begin with that letter. This part can be tricky. Finding questions for X, Z, and Q can be difficult so you might choose to lump some of these together or omit them. The game can be played in a number of ways. For instance, you could begin with "A" and go through the alphabet or allow the students to choose their own questions from any boxcar. Again, this can be done with teams or individuals.

Computer Games

There are a number of excellent, low cost computer games available. "Bible-Q" and "Bible Men" are two that are available through shareware. These can be used in conjunction with parties which you might have for your class in someone's home or if you have access to a computer in the building, the students will love playing them in connection with your class.

Who Am I?

In this simple game, you can have the students do most of the preparation. Assign each student a certain number of Bible characters to research. Give them sufficient time to read about the characters and write a brief description of them. Have each student read his description and then have the class guess who that character is.

Miscellaneous Learning Activities

1. Have older students construct learning aids for the younger students. A model of a typical Palestinian house, a salt-flour map of Canaan, "TV Boxes," maps large enough to place on the floor so that students can follow the journey themselves, and illustrated songbooks are just a few of the possibilities.

2. Have students write and illustrate their own Bible story books.

3. Have students design teaching bulletin boards that deal with the current topic.

4. Make a "This Is Your Life" book for a particular Bible character.

5. Write and illustrate a newspaper about the characters and events surrounding some major Bible event.

6. Have students keep a notebook containing sermon notes, summaries of bulletin articles, reviews of items of current interest from a biblical perspective, and their own applications of current Bible lessons.

"Service Projects"

Students need to learn that Christianity is a doing and serving religion that should have a daily impact on our lives and the lives of others. One way to accomplish this is to arrange "service projects" for the classes. This must be arranged with the cooperation of elders and parents. Here are a few suggestions of what might be done. Be sure to choose a project that is appropriate for your age group.

- Help rake leaves for elderly or at the church building
- Send "thank you" notes to visitors
- Make a "get well" basket for a sick class mate or others
- Visit a nursing home and do something nice for them
- Make greeting cards for the sick and shut-in
- Help clean up around the church building
- Visit the elderly or shut-in and sing for them
- Help with folding or mailing of bulletin

I am sure that you can come up with even better ideas that will be more appropriate for your situation. The object of this is to get the students involved in living their religion.

Conclusion

You are limited only by the boundaries of your own imagination. If you do not feel that you are creative enough to come up with your own games or activities, check with a religious book store and see what they have to offer. Purchased activities do not have to be used exactly as they are. Feel free to adapt them to your specific needs.

The purpose of these activities is not to entertain the students, but to involve them and help them motivate themselves. Learning can be *fun!*

Questions

1. Discuss the purpose and various uses for Bible games and activities. _____
    _____
    _____

2. What are some important things to consider when choosing or creating a game or learning activity? _____
    _____

3. Come up with an idea for a game or learning activity for a particular age group and be prepared to share it with the class._____
    _____

4. Discuss the appropriateness of "service projects." Come up an idea for one and be prepared to share it with the class. _____
    _____
    _____

Lesson 10

Preparing Effective Lesson Plans

Preparation – A Premium

There is no substitute for preparation. If *a teacher fails to plan, he plans to fail!* Perhaps the single most important ingredient to effective teaching is preparing effective lesson plans. Just as a builder needs good blue prints, a teacher needs good lessons plans. They may seem tedious and time consuming at first, but they will give you a structured framework from which to guide your students. Your instruction will need a purpose and direction. Good lesson plans will help provide both of these.

Where to Begin?

The effective teacher will begin preparing for each lesson with prayer. Given the gravity of your responsibility and the knowledge you need to acquire, preparation without prayer is no preparation at all. Do you really think you can do it all alone? It is your task to communicate the Word of God to your students. It just makes sense to begin by talking with the One responsible for that Word.

Five Step Approach to Lesson Plans

1. Read and meditate. Early in the week set aside a quiet time to read the text from which the lesson will come. Make sure that you understand all of the words used in the text. At this point don't worry if you there are some puzzling concepts in the text, just try to get a general grasp of the essential lesson. Follow the example of David and meditate on the text "all the day" (Psl. 119:97). Think about the text. Ponder it. Give it a chance to "soak in." While you sit down, walk, lie down, and rise up (Deut.6:7), think about the importance of this lesson and the most effective approach. No preparation is complete until the teacher also examines himself in light of what is being read. Look at yourself before you look at others.

2. Gain information. While you are meditating on the lesson text, try to gain as much information and insight into the text as possible. Make sure that you know and understand the "facts" of the lesson. This may require reaching into the "teacher's tool pouch." A good concordance, Bible dictionary, additional translations, commentaries, and encyclopedia will prove helpful. Don't forget the human sources available. Talk with more experienced teachers about dif-

ficult texts to gain insight into the meaning and suggestions for effective approaches.

3. Meditate again! Having gained some insight into the meaning and purpose
of the text, meditate once again. Take time to ponder how best to convey the
facts and important lessons of the text. Think about your students. What will
be the most effective approach to take? Out of the lesson, what do they most
need to learn? How can you tie this lesson to what has been learned previously?
Do you want to retell the story as a narrative or retell the story by asking the
students a series of questions? Are there maps, pictures, or other visual aids
that will help you get the message across? Continuing to meditate on the lesson
as you go through the week is a great way to pick up some good illustrations and
applications. You'll be surprised at how practical the lesson can become.

4. Application. What practical applications can be made from this lesson?
How can this lesson change lives and attitudes? This is a very important part
of your preparation. Sterile facts will not impact and change lives. They must
be presented in a context that will help the students see their practicality. For
instance, suppose that you are preparing to teach about the opposition to the
rebuilding of the Temple in Ezra 4. You discover and teach the students that the
opposition came in four forms: compromise, discouragement, fear, and hired
hecklers. Now, what are the students to do with this information? How can it
help them in their daily battle with Satan? Get the point?

5. Polish. Now that you understand the text and its purpose, know how you
are going to present the facts and the application of the lesson, it is time to apply the polish. A good outline (a suggested form will follow) will be helpful and
provide you with the needed structure to keep you on track. Meditate some
more and pray some more. Are you ready to go?

This particular approach to preparing lessons plans is time consuming and
should not be done in one session. Your preparation will be much more effective
if it is spread out over the week. Set aside some quiet time each day to do a little
work on the next lesson. Begin early in the week so that, if unexpected inter-
ruptions occur, you will still have time to do your best. Waiting until Saturday
evening or Sunday morning, will not allow the needed time to do your best.

A Few Additional Considerations While Preparing

Know where the lesson under consideration fits in the overall scheme of the
Bible. If you are using a quarterly or congregational designed curriculum, be able
to relate the lesson to something greater. Every Bible story needs to be presented in some historical context. If you are preparing to teach a lesson on the
sins of Manasseh, you might want to tie him in to the general decline in Judah.
Compare what was happening during his reign to what had gone on in Israel. A
good time line will help you keep the text in its historical context.

When planning your lesson, choose a vocabulary that is appropriate for your age group. Be prepared to define any new words that will be presented in the lesson. If you are uncertain as to whether or not the students understand certain words, don't hesitate to ask them.

Study your lesson well enough that you could explain it in your own words without notes. A teacher that is tethered to an outline or workbook is more likely to lose the interest of the students. Additionally, if you are able to explain the lesson in your own words without the use of notes, then you really understand the lesson!

Plan how to begin and how to end the lesson. Getting the students' attention and interest at the beginning is very significant. Having a planned way to wrap things up is important to the impact of the lesson. Try to have the students leave the room with more on their mind than beating their best friend to the drinking fountain.

Plan extra material. It is much better to have too much than to have too little. Having left over material is better than trying to corral a group of bored or unoccupied students.

Plan your questions ahead of time. In your outline write down the questions that you think are most important. Think back to the lessons on asking good questions and include ones that cause the students to become mentally involved in the lesson.

Your study habits as a teacher are extremely significant. Take a few minutes to check your study habits using the chart on the following page.

Sample Outline for Lesson Plan

I. Introduction
  A. Lesson subject and text:
  B. Purpose of this lesson:
  C. Materials needed for lesson:

II. The Facts of the Lesson
  A. Who:
  B. Where:
  C. When:
  D. Wherefore:
  E. Lesson in the overall scheme of Bible and quarterly.

III. Procedure for Teaching Lesson
  A. Beginning:
  B. Main Points of the lesson:
  C. Activities for reinforcement:
  D. Application:
  E. Close:

Check Your Study Habits			
Question	Seldom or Never	Sometimes	Usually or Always
Do you set aside a certain time for study?			
Do you study other sources than Bible and quarterly?			
Do you make notes as you read?			
Do you look up new terms as you read?			
Do you read carefully and slowly to get the meaning?			
Do you question what others have written before accepting them?			
Do you pray before and after study sessions?			
Do you check to see if you are being effective?			

Questions

1. Why are lessons plans important and what purpose do they serve? _____

   _____

2. Briefly describe what should take place during each of the following steps in lesson plan preparation.
   a. Read/Meditate: _____
   b. Gain information:_____
   c. Meditate again: _____
   d. Application: _____
   e. Polish:_____

3. Summarize additional points to consider when making lesson plans. Be prepared to discuss these in class. _____

   _____

4. Using 1 Samuel 17 as the text prepare a lesson plan for the age group in which you are most interested. In preparing your outline, use the outline suggested in the text.

Lesson 11

Teaching to the Students' Level

Introduction

Successful teaching demands a knowledge of the student as an individual and as a part of a developmental group. While each student in your class is a unique individual with unique abilities and characteristics, he will share certain things in common with others his age. A knowledge of these common characteristics and individual traits is essential for success. Remember, you are not teaching a class, you are teaching students. Get to know them.

Effective teaching requires that the teacher take the students from where they are to where you want them to be. Without a working knowledge of the students individually and developmentally, this will be impossible. How could you give someone directions to Washington, D.C. unless you knew where they were? As a teacher, you need not only to acquire a good working knowledge of God's word, but you also need to gain a good understanding of your students. When these two are coupled, the stage is set for success.

Teaching to the students' level will help you maintain discipline. Teaching that is too easy for students will often be viewed as an insult. If the work is not challenging, the students will tend to get bored and then you have to deal with the paper wad fights that occupy their time. Teaching that is too difficult will discourage the students. Discouraged students will find ways to occupy their time and express their frustration. Seldom will these be productive or pleasant.

Among the things that you need to know about your students are:
- Reading level
- Working vocabulary (oral and reading)
- Writing level
- Spiritual background
- Interests

How Can You Get to Know Your Students?

1. Carefully observe them in the classroom. Make an occasional note about their behavior, attention, interests or other valuable information.

2. Visit them in their homes. This will help you get to know them on a more personal basis.

3. Have them in your home.

4. Observe them before and after services. Observe them at work and at play.

5. Talk with their parents and talk to them.

6. Read and study about their developmental level. You should be able to find some good books at your local library. These will help you get to know their intellectual development and capabilities.

Know Their Learning Style

Not all students learn in the same way. While some may be able to learn in one way, they are capable of learning far more in another style. Knowing the "learning styles" of your students will greatly enhance the effectiveness of your instruction.

Researchers generally suggest three basic learning styles: *visual* (reading), *aural* (listening), and *physical* (actively doing things). Some students learn best by listening to tapes, lectures, or discussions. Others find their learning is promoted more by reading, reviewing notes, scanning books, and the like. Still others feel they learn more through active physical involvement. No one style is better than the other since each has its strengths.

The "Physical Learning Style" (sometimes referred to as Kinesthetic or Tactile) is perhaps the least understood and least valued of the styles. Some students need to be physically involved in the process of learning. Some students need movement in order to learn most efficiently. For instance, when trying to teach a pre-school or lower elementary student a new word or concept, a tactile approach might be most useful. The child might be encouraged to trace the word with his finger while saying it silently. Second the child might trace the word while saying it out loud. Third, if the child is capable of writing, he would write the word from memory and say it out loud. With older students, allowing them to move around the room working at learning stations where they physically do things (such as map puzzles, matching cards which name men and their wives, etc.) will greatly improve their learning. Don't be afraid of movement or noise!

In the interests of effective motivation, it is important to identify each student's learning style as quickly as possible. If, for example, some students seem to learn best by reading, you may want to suggest books for them to read and call on them more often to read aloud. If some students learn best by listening, you may want to play a tape recording of a Bible story being read by someone with a particularly good voice. If some of your students are primarily physical learners, you might encourage them to act out a Bible story or do a puppet show for the younger students.

SQ3R Incorporates Many Learning Styles

Regardless of the particular approach to learning or style of thinking while learning, certain quite practical methods are helpful in consolidating and re-membering information for future use. One of the most practical and widely used methods is the SQ3R system. SQ3R stands for survey, questions, read, recite, and review. This was initially introduced as a study method, but has, over time, proven to be an effective instructional method which incorporates many learning styles.

The SQ3R method involves basically five steps:

1. *Survey.* Begin by skimming through the reading material to get a general overview of the material. It is helpful if the teacher gives the student a general idea of what to look for.

2. *Questions.* Lead the students through several questions designed to address the most important facts and ideas presented. These questions should be very general. (For example, what was Peter's main point in his sermon on Pentecost?) By having the students turn pages and verbalize answers, you involve the visual and aural learning styles.

3. *Read.* Read the answer to your questions. Actively search for it. When you find the answers, write down the answer and where it was found.

4. *Recite.* Have the students retell important events or ideas in their own words.

5. *Review.* Ask the students a series of questions to determine how much they remember. Having them draw lines to connect questions with answers or connect words with something in common (Gospel, prick heart) will involve them physically as well as orally and visually.

If you will be aware of the different learning styles in your classroom and adapt to them, you will be more effective and powerful.

Selected Characteristics
Toddlers (Birth to One):

General Characteristics: Constantly moving, learning to talk, learning through all five senses, limited vocabulary, attention span of no more than a few minutes, requires a great deal of individual attention, tires easily, limited social skills.

Needs: Frequent change of activities, frequent rest times, sense of security, large muscle activities, one teacher or aid for every three or four students, carefully maintained classroom.

Levels of Understanding: Simple brief stories using concepts of God, Jesus, Bible and home. Retell stories often.

Twos and Threes:

General Characteristics: Extremely active, attention span very short, responds to guided play, rapidly growing vocabulary, learns through all five senses, tires easily, forming simple concepts of social interaction, learning to distinguish between right and wrong behaviors, learns by repetition.

Needs: Frequent change of activities, frequent rest periods, consistent discipline, repetition, one teacher or aid for every four to five students.

Level of Understanding: Simple stories (retold in simple language) appreciate Jesus as a friend, the Bible as a special book, and "church time" as a special time, God takes care of them, Jesus as a special friend, learns by singing and through guided play.

Fours and Fives:

General Characteristics: Very active, imitators, attention span growing to about 10 minutes, forming more complex social skills so that they can play with and not just alongside others, big imagination, learning to share, tires easily, curious, growing vocabulary.

Needs: Consistent discipline, stable environment, warm teachers who interact with them, frequent change of activities, one teacher to five or six students.

Level of Understanding: Can begin to grasp simple concepts such as God creating the earth , love of Jesus and desire to please Him; can add new Bible words to verbal vocabulary; can begin to identify with Bible heroes.

Grades One and Two:

General Characteristics: Active and talkative, very imaginative, has developed sufficient social skills to work in small groups, learning to read and write, developing a sense of morality, thinks concretely, eager to learn, emotionally immature, attention span up to 15 minutes.

Needs. Caring teacher who will adapt to emotional and social needs, variety of activities emphasizing involvement, concrete stories and examples, patience, one teacher for seven to ten children.

Level of Understanding: Appreciates the Bible as a special book, begins to gain genuine grasp of love for God and Jesus, beginning to understand what sin is, can apply Bible principles to everyday problems.

Grades Three and Four:

General Characteristics: Energetic, likes group activities, a growing sense of morality, memorizes easily, attention span increases to 15 minutes, increasing sense of self worth and identity, continues to require individual attention, can make application of Bible principles to concrete life situations, possesses an increasing awareness of sin and salvation.

Needs: Variety of activities for involvement, opportunities to pursue individual interests, likes to be a helper in the classroom, their "energy level" requires a teacher with patience, one teacher for ten children.

Level of Understanding: Increasing understanding of chronology makes the "history" of the Bible very important at this level, application of Bible principles to life problems, increasing awareness of what sin is and the need for salvation.

Grades Five and Six:

General Characteristics: Energetic, independent, inquisitive, talkative, imaginative, wants to be like his peers, beginning to think abstractly, likes competition, hero worshiper, memorizes easily, attention span up to 20 minutes.

Needs: Firm and loving discipline, involvement in learning activities, challenges to memorize, competition, good examples of Christian lifestyle, one teacher for 10 students.

Level of Understanding: Application *of* Bible to daily problems, identifying with Bible heroes, challenge to read and investigate areas of interest on own, greater awareness of sin and need for salvation.

Grades Seven-Nine:

General Characteristics: Growing and changing rapidly, extremely self-conscious, independent, peer approval extremely important, capable of abstract thinking, able to reason to solve complex problems, developing his own faith and value system, inquisitiveness leads to doubts, increasing interest in opposite sex.

Needs. Opportunity to make choices and feel a part of classroom management, patient acceptance, teacher who is not easily shocked, challenging material, firm discipline, good Christian role models.

Level of Understanding: Understanding and application of biblical principles in life, knowledge of sin and need for salvation, interrelationships of Bible material.

Grades Ten-Twelve:

General Characteristics: Independent, rapidly increasing abilities, sometimes a "know-it-all," emotional, doubts, settling on own faith and value system, strong peer influence, can reason and solve complex problems, cliquish.

Needs: Caring teachers who supervise while allowing independence, challenging material, challenge to serve, opportunities to express doubts and seek answers without criticism, guidance regarding relationships with opposite sex.

Level of Understanding: Understanding and application of biblical principles in life, knowledge of sin and need for salvation, interrelationships of Bible material.

Questions

1. Why is it important to know students as individuals and as part of a development group? _____

   _____

2. What are some possible effects of teaching or not teaching to the student's
   level?_____

   _____

3. Discuss the suggestions of how to get to know your students. _____

   _____

   Which are most practical? _____
   Least practical?_____
   What other ideas do you have? _____

   _____

4. List the three learning styles discussed and describe each. _____

   _____

   _____

   _____

   How would these affect the way you presented a lesson? _____

   _____

   _____

   _____

   _____

5. Discuss the use of SQ3R in a Bible class. _____

   _____

6. Take a closer look at the students in your congregation. How are they divided? _____

   _____

   How could this be improved? _____

   _____

7. Choose a particular age group other than the one with which you are most
   familiar and develop a lesson plan for the story of Jonah for that age group.
   Try to incorporate all three learning styles. In class compare your plans with
   those of other age groups._____

   _____

   _____

   _____

   _____

   _____

Motivation in the Classroom

"Follow Me, and I will make you fishers of men" (Matt. 4:19).

"Come unto Me, all you who labor and are heavy laden, and I will give you rest" (Matt. 12:28).

"In My Father's house are many mansions; if it were not so, I would have told you. I go to prepare a place for you. And if I go and prepare a place for you, I will come again and receive you to Myself" (Jn. 14:2-4).

On numerous occasions, Jesus motivated His disciples with the promise of reward. He promised to be with them, bless them, guide them, and reward their faithful labor. He appealed to their need for intrinsic and extrinsic motivation. They needed motivation if they were to successfully take the gospel into a world that was hostile to them. The unseen and the unexperienced had to become real to them. They needed motivation.

The students in your classroom are no different from the disciples that Jesus left behind. How many times have you faced a group of students with glazed eyes and dull minds? Yet, this same group of students can become a group of intellectual dynamos when properly motivated. I do not believe that you as the teacher can motivate them; that is something that they must do for themselves. But, you can create an environment in which self-motivation is possible and encouraged.

What Is Motivation?

Motivation is sometimes called the "go" of personality, an apt description since the absence of motivation usually reduces most normal people to a state of listless apathy. Although motivation cannot be seen directly, it can be inferred from the behavior that we ordinarily refer to as "ability." While our observation of another person's ability denoted what an individual can do or is able to do, "motivation" tends to summarize our observations as to what a person wants to do. As you know from experience, motivation and ability are not necessarily re-lated. All in all, what a person wants to do can be a powerful factor in achieving his or her goals. You might think of motivation as being the engine power that energizes and directs behavior.

Motives are related to motivation in the sense that they refer to the needs or desires that cause us to act and, hence, feel motivated, in the first place. Motives serve three important and overlapping functions that include:

1. Energizing us (getting us started).
2. Directing us (pointing us in the right direction).
3. Helping us select the behavior most appropriate for achieving our goals.

The feeling of being motivated, then, is a psychological state of mind that is the consequence of people activating their motives.

Two Kinds of Motivation

If a student works hard to win the praise of their parents, gain the teacher's praise, or win a game, his motivation is primarily extrinsic. His reasons for work lie primarily outside of himself. If, on the other hand, a student works hard because he enjoys the Bible and desires to learn it, his motivation is primarily intrinsic. His reasons for learning and hard work reside primarily inside himself.

Most teachers recognize the need for intrinsic motivation. It is self-starting, self-perpetuating, and requires only an inward interest to keep the motivational machinery going.

However, extrinsic motivation is what most students (and teachers!) have in the backs of their minds when they think about what happens in everyday classroom situations. It is often important in getting students started in the first place and keeping them on track. However, when it is over stressed and over used, it tends to encourage somewhat shallow, answer-oriented thinking designed more to please the teacher than to reach a deeper understanding of the material at hand.

Both kinds of motivation are important in the operation of a classroom – extrinsic motivators get things started while intrinsic motivators sustain the learning process. Tangible rewards are important, especially with younger children, but a teacher's verbal or written acknowledgement of a good job or fine effort are more likely to be incorporated by students into their own inner feelings of satisfaction. This has the effect of encouraging the self-perpetuating energy behind intrinsic motivation.

Seven Proven Motivators That Really Work!

In the *Master Teacher* (Vol. 23:2) Robert DeBruyn listed the following seven motivators. They are relatively easy to understand and learn. However, it may take years of experience to successfully and consistently incorporate them into our individual classrooms.

Personal gain is without question, the single most powerful motivator. Whenever we try to get students to do anything, they consciously or unconsciously ask themselves, "What's in it for me?" If the answer is nothing, our efforts to motivate will be severely hindered. When we ask students to work hard or learn for us rather than for themselves, we automatically lose the force of this powerful motivator.

Prestige is another motivator. We all know how prestige motivates young people to be in a certain group or wear certain clothing. How can we make working hard and doing well in our Bible classes prestigious for students? We must make our classrooms important places to be. The attitude of the teacher and the parents will set the tone for the importance of Bible classes. Consistent attendance and reinforcement at home will help students understand the importance of the Bible class. Being successful in Bible class will be prestigious, if it is perceived as n portant.

Pleasure is an important motivator for students and teachers. Remember, learning and improving are pleasurable. This doesn't mean that Bible classes must always be fun and games. It doesn't mean that discipline problems should be ignored. However, it does mean that the atmosphere in the classroom must be pleasant and cheerful. A teacher who is moody, unpleasant, or tries to make the work too hard, kills positive motivation.

Security is a strong motivator. For some students, it is the strongest force in their lives. If we want to motivate students, we must make them feel secure with us, their classmates, and the work being done. It is inevitable that students will give wrong answers to questions. How do you respond? The effective teacher will focus on the content of the *answer* when correcting and not the student. You can thank the student for trying, show appreciation for his thought or willingness to answer, while looking for the correct *answer*. Search for non- threatening, non-destructive ways to reply to incorrect answers and thereby help build an environment of security. A student's hesitance to try is often a result of his desire to avoid fear and failure. We can counter this by assuring the students that they will find acceptance, success, and security in our classrooms.

Convenience means making work and procedures as simple as possible. Aren't you as a consumer motivated by convenience? I often shop where I do and buy what I buy because it is convenient. In our classrooms is learning convenient? We need to focus more on student convenience than teacher convenience. When giving instructions, designing assignments, and conducting discussions, we need to focus on the convenience of the learning experience.

New experiences can also be used to motivate students. If we change the pace, alter routines, and take new approaches to teaching lessons, motivation can be enhanced.

Finally, *love* is a motivator. It is easy to see why. It is the only emotion humans can't live without. Students must have it, and so must we. That's why the teacher who tries to motivate without caring will find resistance. Jesus used love to motivate His disciples when He told them, "If you love Me, you will keep my commandments" (Jn. 14:15).

Communicate High Expectations

The effective teacher is one who honestly believes that all students can learn and so they insist that all learn. They believe that all students can behave and achieve to the degree that the teacher expects them to behave and achieve. They avoid any action which communicates low expectations.

How could a teacher cause a student to lower his expectations?

- By failing to be positive about learning.
- Not listening to the students. This tells them that we don't care. By quickly moving to another student when the first doesn't respond immediately to our question.
- By praising the class rather then individuals. The class as a whole will at times be deserving of praise, but every student needs personal praise.
- By constantly giving blanket criticisms of the class.
- Using terms such as fast, slow, dumb, and smart when referring to students establishes a range of expectations within that student when they are probably very capable.
- By giving insincere or undeserved praise. This cheapens the effectiveness of our praise.

There is a direct correlation between conveying high expectations and student achievement.

Conclusion

Just as there is more than one way for learning to occur, there is more than one way to stimulate and enhance student motivation. Some students, we know, are driven by strong inner drives to learn and achieve, while others function best when working for reasons or goals that are outside or extrinsic to their inner states. Some students are spurred on by praise and other expressions of positive reinforcement, while others work hardest when their work is more critically appraised.

It is not easy to assess the degree to which students are motivated. Bible classrooms are not neatly divided into the sleepers and hand wavers. Sometimes the most involved students are the ones who say hardly a word, but who, in actuality, are deeply caught up in the ideas and thoughts related to what is happening. They are not unmotivated, but merely quiet.

All in all, Bible classroom motivation and human learning is a three-dimensional process that includes the content at hand, the student, and the teacher, Each plays a part. Motivating students is not a gift reserved only for the super

Motivation Mini-Clinic	
Why Student May Be Unmotivated	**Some Things You Can Do About It**
Subject is boring	Make more interesting by the inclusion of learning games. Supply incentives.
Student won't exert self	Specficy objectives, rewards, try to make their lack of effort non-prestigious
Student is less capable than others in class	Give him more personal attention and help; give him different kinds of assignments; work to strengthen his self-confidence
Student does not have a good spiritual background	Get to know him on a more personal basis; without calling attention to what you are doing, have more experienced students help by reviewing basic facts
Lack of support from parents	Become a prime source of encouragement for student; encourage him to learn for his own sake
Student is afraid to try because of fear of failure	Arrange a series of attainable goals; help the student to achieve them
Student sees no need for Bible knowledge	Make your lessons practical; use frequent examples from daily life to show how Bible knowledge impacts daily life; present more than isolated facts

teacher with built-in charisma, but is the consequence of hard work, careful planning, and a deep concern for the ultimate expression of growth and potential in each student.

Questions

1. Discuss Jesus' use of rewards as a means of motivating His disciples. _____

_____

_____

2. Define motivation. _____

_____

_____

3. Discuss the statement, "Teachers cannot motivate students. They can only

create an environment in which the students can motivate themselves." Do you agree? _____
Disagree? _____

4. Define the two kinds of motivation. _____
    _____
    _____

    Why are both needed in Bible classrooms?_____
    _____

5. What are some potential dangers when a teacher over-emphasizes one kind of motivation to the exclusion of the other?_____
    _____

6. List DeBruyn's seven proven motivators. Give an example of how a Bible class teacher could incorporate each in his Bible class.
    a. _____
    b. _____
    c. _____
    d. _____
    e. _____
    f. _____

7. What effect does a teacher's expectations have on student motivation? ___
    _____

8. Discuss the role of content, student, and teacher in the process of motivation. _____
    _____
    _____

Evaluation of the Learning Process

Evaluation is the profitable process that involves making a qualitative judgment of "how good" or "how effective" a teacher and student have performed. Evaluations are usually subjective, personal, and difficult to define with a high degree of precision. Simply put, to evaluate something means to place a value on it based on previously determined standards. Without honest evaluation on the part of the teacher and student no improvements in the process can take place and past mistakes cannot be overcome.

Evaluation can be a significant dimension of the total learning process when it encourages the teacher and student to see how they can improve their performance. It will permit the teacher to assimilate and interrelate as much evidence as he can about how his students learn. It will also encourage teachers to do a bit of honest "soul-searching" regarding their role in the learning process.

Evaluation is just as necessary as thorough preparation. The growing, effective teacher consciously evaluates the lesson content, presentation, and learning environment. Taking his sacred responsibility seriously, he evaluates himself, his pupils, and the lesson. His evaluation may be known only to God, but it will be reflected indelibly and eternally upon the hearts and lives of his students.

For the Bible class teacher, evaluation of learning takes on particular significance when weighed in the balances of eternity. The student's eternal destiny will, in part, be shaped by how and what you teach. Therefore, it must be taken seriously. Determining the students' spiritual understanding and attitudes is of paramount importance. What progress has been made must be determined in order to properly map out future progress. The Bible class teacher needs to know if his teaching has been effective and his preparation adequate.

What Was My Purpose?

Effective teachers will be able to answer two basic questions about every lesson they present:

1. Why did I teach this lesson?

2. How did I want my students to benefit from this lesson?

These two questions must be understood before the lesson begins and will form the basis of the evaluation.

A Bible class teacher's objectives can usually be broken down into three major classes:

1. Informational goals and objectives. This would include learning and mastering such things as names, dates, technical terms, definitions, principles, concepts, and so on.

2. Proficiency goals and objectives. Some examples of proficiencies or skills here might include being able to quickly find specific passages, use of basic facts to formulate doctrinal arguments, and so on.

3. Attitudinal goals and objectives. This is a more difficult arena of evaluation because it involves matters of personal preference and personal value. It would include such things as an appreciation and love for God, understanding of the grossness of sin, and the severity of man's need for salvation.

All three of these kinds of goals should be the object of evaluation. Since each is dissimilar and expressed differently, they will require divergent approaches to evaluation.

How Do I Evaluate Myself?

The effective and secure teacher is not afraid to carefully, prayerfully, and honestly evaluate his performance in the Bible classroom. Ask yourself a series of questions designed to make you more aware of the conditions in your classroom and your students' performance. Was it a good lesson? Was it appropriate for this age group? Were my goals and objectives clear to me and accomplished with the students? Did I address the needs of this individual group? Did the students seem to be interested? Did they gain the knowledge and display the attitudes which were targeted? What would I do differently next time? How could you have improved this lesson? Were the students excited when they left? Did I do the best that I could? These and other questions will help to focus your attention on the quality and effectiveness of the lesson.

In addition to these general questions, you need to ask yourself some specific questions relating to the content of the lesson:

1. Did I thoroughly know the lesson that I was to teach?

2. Did I use words that were easily understood by the students? Did I take the time to carefully define new words?

3. Did I begin with what they already knew to capture their attention, and then move on to the new material?

4. Did I require the students to reproduce, in some way, the lesson in their own words?

5. Did I review past lessons and bring the lesson to closure?

You also need to check for strengths and weaknesses in your manner of presentation.

1. Did you speak with an animated voice using voice inflections for emphasis or were you monotone?

2. Did you use appropriate gestures or were they weak, stiff, or unnatural?

3. Did you use proper grammar and pronunciation?

4. Did you establish and maintain eye contact with the students or did you carry on a conversation with the floor?

5. Did you display any annoying mannerisms such as clearing your throat, jerking at clothing, leaning or rocking on a podium, or anything similar to this that might distract the students?

6. Did you show emotion with your face?

How did you do? Would you like to have yourself for a teacher?

How Do I Evaluate My Students?

Effective teachers do not evaluate students as a means of punishment or embarrassment. Seldom will you motivate lazy students in Bible classes by giving them tests or quizzes. You evaluate your students in order to enhance the learning process. Any evaluation that occurs for any other reason will not facilitate effective learning.

I am not persuaded that giving tests and quizzes in Bible class is the best way to evaluate the progress of students. In some cases it may be effective and appropriate, but as a general rule, I am convinced that they will be counterproductive.

There are a number of other ways that evaluation can take place. For instrance, many attitudinal objectives are best evaluated by observation. Do the students enjoy coming to Bible class? Are they prepared? Do they express respect for the Lord and the Bible? Keep your eyes and ears open for signs of their attitudes. No student can successfully keep them hidden forever!

Effective teachers are often sneaky! You can use a game as a tool of evaluation. A "Bible Bee," "Twenty Questions," or other games mentioned in chapter 9 will provide opportunities to evaluate the students grasp of basic facts. Asking students to evaluate various life situations will help you determine whether or not they can make application of what they have learned. Questions such as,

"What do you think should be done in this situation?", "If someone tells you that _____ is ok to do, how would you answer them?", "How would you go about persuading someone that he needed to do this or that?", or "How do you think a particular Bible character would handle this situation?" will all provide the students with an opportunity to display their genuine grasp of the principles of the lesson.

Remember, if the students have not learned, you have not taught. You will not not know if they have learned unless you evaluate!

Questions

1. Develop a ten question instrument that could be used by a teacher to evaluate his performance. Share these with the class.

2. Develop a ten question instrument that could be used to evaluate the students' performance. Share these with the class.

Teach.
Teach well.
Teach to glorify God.

Epilogue

The Greatest of These. . .

Though I have all the Elmer's glue and scissors and have read the lesson five times and have not love, I am not a teacher.

And though I have all the construction paper, glitter, and Bible posters, puzzles, and unit activities, and have been in a special planning session, and have not love, I am not a teacher.

For being a teacher is more than being on time, present, Bible in hand, and a lesson prepared. It's even more than faithfully attending the church services.

A teacher is kind and smiles a lot.

A teacher looks neat and is not easily provoked when something is wrong with the heating or cooling system.

A teacher is not envious of other's talents, but uses his/her own creativity and talents to the best of his/her ability.

A teacher seeketh not for his/her name to be praised, but works for the glory of God.

They beareth the problems, believeth and hopeth the best for all the children they teach, for a teacher's work is in vain unless they have true interest in the children.

Where there be magic markers, they shall dry up.

Where there be chalk and blackboards, they shall crumble. Where there be printed literature, it shall fade.

But a right relationship to God will endure forever, as it is shared in the lives of your children.

All work is a result of His love.

And now abideth planning, preparation, and love, these three. But the greatest of these is love.

For without God's love all work is for naught.

(The author of this beautiful poem is not known. I found it in *Let's Be Great Teachers,* by *Sue* Crabtree.)

References

Biehler, R., & Snowman, J. (1982). *Psychology Applied to Teaching.* Houghton Mifflin Co., Boston.

Cauley, K., Linder, F., and McMillan, J. (1991). *Educational Psychology 91/92.* Duskin Publishing Group, Guilford, CN.

Cole, M., and Cole, S. (1989). *The Development of Children.* Scientific American Books, New York.

Crabtree, S. (   ). *Let's Be Great Teachers.* Bible and School Supply, Montgomery, AL.

Hamachek, D. (1985). *Psychology in Teaching, Learning, and Growth.* Allyn and Bacon, Boston.

Leavitt, G., and Daniel, E. (1989). *Teach With Success.* Standard Publishing, Cincinnati, OH.

Miller, R., and Miller C. (1979). *Up the Stairway of Teaching.* Miller Publications, Orlando, FL.

Richards, L. (1970). *Creative Bible Teaching.* Moody Press, Chicago.

Swain, D. (1964). *Teach Me to Teach.* Judson Press, Valley Forge, PA.

Waldron, B., and Waldron, S. (1990). *A Generation That Knows Not God.* Bob Waldron, Pinson, AL.

CPSIA information can be obtained at www.ICGtesting.com
Printed in the USA
LVOW120659130613

338385LV00004B/62/P